Other Books by Barbara Ensrud

American Vineyards

Wine with Food

The Pocket Guide to Cheese

The Pocket Guide to Wine

Best Wine Buys for $10 or Less

Villard Books
New York
1991

Best Wine Buys for $10 or Less

A Guide for the Frugal Connoisseur Featuring Wines from Around the World

Barbara Ensrud

VILLARD BOOKS is a registered trademark
of Random House, Inc.

Library of Congress Cataloging-in-Publication Data
Ensrud, Barbara.
Best wine buys for $10 or less: a guide for the
frugal connoisseur featuring wines from around
the world/Barbara Ensrud.
p.   cm.   ISBN 0-679-73918-1
1. Wine and wine making.   I. Title.   II. Title: Best wine
buys for $10 or less: a guide for the frugal connoisseur
featuring wines from around the world
TP548.E559   1991   641.2'2'0296—dc20   90-47690

Manufactured in the United States of America
9 8 7 6 5 4 3 2 1
First edition

Book design by J. K. Lambert

For

Allen and Marily,

Betty and Gil,

Bob and Kay

Acknowledgments

I wish to express special thanks to my agent, Charlotte Sheedy, who saw the need for this book and prodded me to do it; and to my editor, Emily Bestler, for her enthusiasm, patience, and guidance in bringing the project to fruition.

Many years of contacts throughout the wine world have made this book possible. I am grateful to all of them, and especially to those who are dedicated to providing good wine at moderate prices for the American wine drinker.

Contents

Introduction

Recently I attended a lunch at the apartment of
a Manhattan designer. As we visited over hors
d'oeuvres, our host poured a crisp, fresh, very
pleasant white wine. The guests, no strangers to
good wine, all remarked on how appealing it
was, and were surprised to learn that it was a
dry Muscat from Portugal. It made a wonderful
aperitif.

A little later the wine served with lunch—this
time in a chilled clay carafe—was another palate pleaser. Conversation literally stopped
when one of the guests asked what it was. The
designer, with a sly smile, remarked that it was
a Chardonnay from Chile. Most of the guests
had never heard of it; they had no idea, in fact,
that countries like Chile even produced Chardonnay. They were even more surprised to
learn how inexpensive the wines were—$5 or
$6 a bottle—and eager to know where they
could buy them. Everyone agreed that they
were tired of paying $14 or $15 for wines that
weren't nearly as drinkable as the much lower-
priced wines their host was serving.

Drinking good wine can be a wallet-busting
proposition these days, but it doesn't have to
be. It's fine to splurge on $15, $20, or $40 wines
when you feel like it, or when a special occasion

merits it, but if you like to drink wine fairly regularly, prices like that can mount up to a small fortune fast. Even owners of lavish cellars like to know of bargains for everyday drinking. I know people whose cellars are such that they could pull forth a Château Lafite or Cheval-Blanc—mature and ready to drink—every night of the week. Truly great wines like these are serious and dramatic; they demand attention, you don't just quaff them down—you have to take note of all the complexities of aroma and character that make them the rare and costly creatures that they are. Even the owners of wonderfully stocked cellars aren't necessarily in the mood for an eventful wine *every* night.

Great wines can provide thrilling moments for the wine lover. (In fact, I insist on such moments at least once a week!) Most of us, however, are not looking for a "Great Experience" every time we open a bottle. We just want something that tastes good with our food, something that is enjoyable to drink. Some bargain wines can be more than that, though—like the spectacular $6 Cabernet from Chile that's more drinkable than some Bordeaux at thrice the price, or the Italian Rosso di Montalcino that costs a third of what its more illustrious cousin goes for.

Wine-pricing is capricious, and often bears no relation to the quality of what is inside the bottle. A lot of wineries—in this country and abroad—arbitrarily set the price of a given bottle based on how they want it to be perceived by the public and by critics, regardless of the quality of the grapes used to make it. Image-pricing, it's called. By the same token, there are excellent wines available that are underrated, wines that simply can't command the higher prices their quality merits. Such are the ways of the marketplace—it teems with quite ordinary stuff selling at highly inflated prices, while wine just as good, sometimes better, can be had for a song.

Price is, in fact, a spurious guide to drinking well. You don't always get what you pay for, and it's easy to make mistakes if you don't know what you're doing. This is as true for cheap wines as for those that are expensive or over-priced. There are hundreds of wines available for under $10, and dozens priced at $2.99 to $5.99 a bottle. Much of it is dreck.

Some of it, however, is very good indeed—in fact, it's amazing the number of good, drinkable wines available, all well under $10. This book is an attempt to separate the wheat from the chaff —concentrating, of course, on the *wheat,* the good stuff, the *consistently* good stuff.

This book's approach differs from those of other buying guides in two significant ways. First, it discusses types of wine and recommends producers rather than individual bottles of a specific vintage, and, second, there are no numerical ratings.

I find it frustrating to read guides that rate wines of a given vintage only to find that the wines in question are actually no longer available. This is especially true of inexpensive wines, most of which are intended for drinking when they come on the market. By the time the book is out, a new vintage has appeared. It's different with more expensive wines like classified Bordeaux; several vintages of Château Haut-Brion or Palmer, say, are often available simultaneously. In any case such wines are usually bought and cellared, so that individual vintage ratings for a specific wine have validity over a long period of time.

I have chosen instead to recommend wines

that are of reliable quality on a consistent basis. Of what use is it to recommend the Beaulieu 1988 Beau Tour Cabernet Sauvignon when the wine that will be in stores when this book is published will be the '89? Or, if you read it a year from now, the '90?

It seems to me much more useful to know that, year in and year out, BV Beau Tour is an excellent buy—you don't have to buy a new edition of this guide next year to know that. This is true for a great many wines in the $10-and-under range because the producers recommended strive for consistent style and quality year to year. This book will not be totally out of date in a year—unless all herein suddenly cave in to compromise and mediocrity. Not likely, I'm thinking.

As for numerical ratings, I know they provide a quick clue to a wine's quality, but I've never really liked the notion of reducing wine to a cipher. It wouldn't work with this format anyway, since such ratings must be for individual wines of a given vintage. Everything recommended here offers good-to-excellent drinking. The information I offer is really only a starting point, because new wines at this level are coming onto the market all the time.

The book is arranged geographically by country, and subdivided either by region or wine type, whichever is most appropriate. In France and Italy, for example, each region is treated separately. In California the wines are categorized by varietal (or type)—Chardonnay, for example, with some wines singled out for special comment.

It gives me great pleasure to share the discoveries I've made through persistent tasting. If you keep up with newsletters and peruse wine periodicals and weekly wine columns in your local newspaper, many of these wines will already be familiar to you. Those of you who enjoy good wine but don't always have the time or inclination to chase after the various sources of information, however, may find yourselves referring to this guide frequently. Look up the wine you're curious about—if the name is under Recommended Producers, it's because the wine has proven consistently good and you can buy with confidence.

My objective here is to concentrate on great wine buys for $10 and under. Consequently some very nice wines don't make the cut—Dolcetto for $11 instead of the $5 or $6 that it used to be; ditto certain Barbera d'Alba and Pinot Grigio, as well as some Chardonnays, Merlots, and Zinfandels from California. Interestingly, though, the competition for shelf space and pressure to sell (there really is an awful lot of wine out there) brings on some surprising price reductions. Many of the wines that at full markup would be $12 or $14 can often be found for $10 or less. This is where it pays to seek out a compatible wineshop. Read on.

HOW TO USE THIS BOOK

Within each country the wines are listed according to how they are best known—in some cases by region (such as Bordeaux), in others by grape variety (Chardonnay), type (Rosso di Montalcino), occasionally by producer (Boutari), whichever is the most informative. A few symbols indicate special situations as follows:

- ✪ Superbuy, outstanding wine for the price
- ✳ Excellent value
- ♦ Wines that at full markup would be over $10 but are frequently found marked down or discounted
- ♥ Perceptible sweetness in wine types normally considered dry, such as Chardonnay
- ■ No oak

For unfamiliar terms, check the Glossary, page 159.

Best Wine Buys for $10 or Less

The Wineshop of the 1990s

The decade of the nineties looks as if it is shaping up—or at least starting out—in favor of consumers: huge inventories of wine from a series of the remarkably good vintages of the eighties. As long as the pipeline is full, there will be pressure in the market to move wine—prices, particularly for wines in the $10 to $15 range, may well soften over the next few years, putting better wines back within reach of everyday drinking. People are drinking less, and while it is true that they are trading up, there is a limit to what they will spend on a regular basis.

One of the things I strongly encourage everyone to do is to make more intelligent—and enjoyable—use of a good wineshop. It's there for you, make it work for you. Too many consumers are intimidated by wineshops. Confronted by thousands of bottles, they have no idea how to go about choosing a wine. Usually they settle for a familiar name, or one they've seen advertised or heard about from a friend. Normally assertive people can turn timid in a wineshop, afraid to appear ignorant or unsophisticated. In some stores, it is true, the staff can be dismissive if you aren't looking for $40 Bordeaux or $20 Cabernets. Attitudes are changing, though, and the better stores are making every effort to become user-friendly.

The nineties will mark a new era in wine retailing. It's already under way. The last two decades have seen the evolution of liquor store into wineshop—it may be a huge warehouse like Sam's in Chicago or Trader Joe in Los Angeles, or swank boutiques like Morrell in Manhattan and The Wine Merchant of Beverly Hills. Often it's a wine-and-food emporium like Martin Wine Cellar in New Orleans, Irvine Market in Beverly Hills, or Cirace in Boston, where you can shop for dinner *and* the wine to go with it. Today, every major metropolitan area has at least one and probably several such stores (see the list of wine stores by city in the appendix, page 161), which stock an amazing choice of wines. Even smaller cities and suburban areas now have good wineshops. They get better as store personnel learn more about wine and discover the rewards of being as helpful to customers as they can—steering them to good values, helping to match wine with menus for entertaining, and making them feel welcome and at home in the store.

Whatever its size, atmosphere, or decor, the wineshop of today has become a center of wine-oriented activity, a lively source of information and exchange. In states where on-premise tasting is permitted, retailers often hold regular tastings. By all means, check this out in your area; tasting is unquestionably the best way to find out what you really like. If your local shop holds regular tastings, it can be a wonderful way to experiment with new wines—expensive ones as well as bargains. At Schaefer's in the suburbs of Chicago, for instance, Saturday afternoon tastings always include some of the better, more expensive wines. In December, Calvert-Woodley Liquors in Washington, D.C., holds weekend wine tastings, pouring several of the top brands. These are very popular events; people try a broad range of Champagnes, exchange views about them, browse about the store for other holiday needs, and have a great time.

GET TO KNOW YOUR WINE MERCHANT

Wine merchants are a lot more knowledgeable than they used to be. A good wine merchant tastes constantly—probably as much as most wine writers do—knows his product, and makes sure his staff is knowledgeable, too. He (or she) can be a great resource. Don't be intimidated because you feel you don't know a lot about wine. If he has any sense of salesmanship, he will want to steer you to the best possible values for your money so you will come back. Yes, he undoubtedly has plenty of customers who spend a lot of money on wine, but he cannot rely on big spenders alone. He needs a broad clientele that keeps coming back. Besides, you may one day be a bigger customer than you are now.

Keeps coming back is a key phrase: It's why he needs to try to please you. In a national survey of wineshops most merchants said that what they wanted to be known for was *service,*

so let's hold them to it. If someone is dismissive
or intimidates you in any way, confront him
with it, or go to another store and perhaps explain *why* you left the other one. If there isn't
another, complain to your local wine writer, or
write *The Wine Spectator* (or write to me).

The new breed of wine retailers, however,
recognizes that customers who are pleased with
the guidance they get begin to take more interest in wine and become eager to try different
wines and broaden their horizons. It can be very
useful to establish a kind of rapport with a retailer or someone on the staff. As they get to
know what you like and what your wine requirements are, they can more readily suggest
the kinds of wines that would please you.

Wilfred Wong, whose family owns the Ash-
bury Market in San Francisco, says it all comes
down to a matter of trust. "The bottom line is
trust," says Wong. "If people don't trust what
you stock, then forget it. People get suspicious
when they see a wine marked down, for instance. 'What's wrong with it?' they ask. If you
want a loyal clientele, you have to taste the
wines yourself, so you know what you're offering and can stand behind it."

USING YOUR WINESHOP:
WHAT TO LOOK FOR

Specials and Markdowns. Wineshops like to
feature specials, especially if they advertise in
the local newspaper. Sometimes these are
called loss leaders, wines the store makes little
or no profit on just to attract attention—the
prospect of a bargain always lures customers. I
saw Masi's Campo Fiorin, usually $9 or more at

full markup, for $6.99 in one shop—it's a good buy at $9 but a real Superbuy at $7.

Even the best shops will eventually mark down wines they can't move—like '87 Bordeaux or wines that may be very good but didn't quite catch on. Sometimes there are real gems to be had.

But *whoa!* I am *not* saying that all wines on special are good buys. *Far from it.* A 1983 Hermitage for $8? An '84 Meursault for $10? Beware. These wines normally cost three times those amounts. If either is really good, chances are the retailer would have quietly mentioned it to one of his best customers who he knows love Meursault. Not invariably, of course; maybe it really is a terrific wine, and a great buy. If it isn't, and he values you as a customer, he will steer you to something better at the same price.

I actually saw in one reputable Manhattan wineshop, in 1990, a bin of 1979 Côtes-du-Rhône. 1979? Totally puzzled, I asked the proprietor about it. Côtes-du-Rhône is usually a wine to drink within two to three years, maybe six or seven for Guigal (the top producer), but eleven!?? He looked a little embarrassed and admitted that a distributor had "discovered" a couple of leftover cases sitting around, and he had bought it for fifty cents on the dollar. Interesting, I thought, and he's selling it for $5.99 a bottle. "Is it any good?" I asked. Again, slight hesitation. "Well," he said, with a shrug, "it's a little tired."

By the same token I have seen four- to five-year-old Beaujolais, or even Beaujolais *nouveau,* believe it or not, sitting around on sale. Even at $2.99, this is no deal. It's old, it's tired, it's lost its fruit. I would venture to say, in fact, beware of anything on sale for $3 or less. It could be all right—certainly some of the Romanian, Bulgarian, or Yugoslavian table wines that go for that amount are perfectly decent, if not great. But always try a bottle before you buy such a wine in quantity.

Direct Imports. Some retailers travel to wine regions regularly and seek out wines they can import directly and offer to their customers as an exclusive at low prices. These can be excellent value for casual occasions or for large parties. Sherry-Lehmann in Manhattan, one of the first shops in this country to specialize in wine way back in the 1950s, has had enormous success for years with its $4.79 Cler Blanc, a delightful little quaff from the Loire Valley. Recently they added an agreeable "house" red made in the Rhône Valley, which they sell for the same reasonable price. Some shops make it a point to have several such wines; they are worth checking out, and often more interesting and stylish than jug wines.

In-Store Tastings. Attend these regularly if you can, *if* you find them helpful and fun. They should be both. Such events are not legal in some states, unfortunately. In others, wineshops can sponsor such events or hold them jointly with a restaurant, but they aren't permitted in the store itself.

Newsletters. Get on the mailing list. Many wineshops publish catalogs or newsletters that are enormously helpful in letting you know about new arrivals, special sales, new books, tastings, wine dinners, and other events. Most newsletters are informative. Some are very amusing and entertaining—like the one put out by Glenn Bardgett and Geoffrey Brooke of the Wine Cellar in St. Louis. Punsters, these two, but I laugh as much as I groan at some of their wordplay on wine names.

Some shops also have wine books, newsletters by wine critics, and other periodicals available for customers to peruse. Take a look, if they do; it's a good way to pick up tips on what's new and what's hot.

Half-bottles. Always check out the half-bottle section. It may well offer the opportunity for something good that costs twice as much for a full bottle. For instance, $9 or $10 can get you one of those Chardonnays, Cabernets, Bordeaux, or Rhônes that sell for $15 to $20 in a 750-milliliter bottle. It is now legal to sell 500 milliliter (half-liter) bottles, which will give two people two generous glasses each. The 500s haven't quite caught on yet, but are likely to become very popular with consumers.

Wineries, restaurants, and wineshops often consider half-bottles a nuisance, requiring special handling and extra expense. But they offer just the right amount on occasion—especially for singles but also for couples who maybe just want to enjoy one glass each with dinner on a week night.

It's important to know, however, that half-bottles age faster than regular bottles—anything that's been around too long could well be fading or over the hill. Don't buy a half-bottle of four-year-old Muscadet, for example. Again, ask about the wine if you aren't sure—and if it turns out to be disappointing, tell the store. Or take it back the next day. I know it's not easy to do that, but you don't have to make a scene.

Express surprise that it wasn't good, and ask the owner or salesman if he knows why.

Browse. Take time to browse in wineshops when you can, whether you're prepared to buy at that moment or not. The owner won't mind, and it's very instructive. You begin to get familiar with wine names (which most consumers say is their biggest problem: They can't remember the names of the wines they've tasted somewhere and liked). You observe what people are buying, hear what's being recommended. Chances are you'll even see a bottle or two you want to try—and do it. As long as you're not spending a fortune, it's the best possible way to discover what you like and what you *don't* like —which is also important.

Buying Wine. Whenever you can, buy by the case, especially if you are buying a wine you know you like. A great opportunity to do so is when you're buying for a party. Buy a few more bottles than you actually need. If you do this periodically, you will find yourself building a modest collection before you know it. You'll soon see how handy it is to have wine on hand when the right moment presents itself unexpectedly. You might want to buy a case of all the same wine, or a mixed case of three or four different wines, or six different ones. Buying this way lets you get ahead of the game a bit, so that you don't get caught short and have to make an emergency run to the wine store. There are other advantages as well—it can be cheaper, for instance. If the wine isn't already on sale, you may get up to 10 percent off for buying a case, the equivalent of a free bottle.

Discount Stores. No question about it, wine prices are rising across the board, especially imports. Strong economies in Europe, a weaker American dollar, and an increased global demand for good wine have all contributed to the situation, which is likely to continue through the decade. Discount stores provide a kind of buffer against this. Because they buy in such huge quantities, they can afford to cut their profit margins per bottle. This makes a huge difference sometimes in wines priced from $8 to $15. The savings can be somewhat less on more expensive wines. For Bordeaux and Burgundy, in fact, nondiscount stores may offer better buys, particularly on first offerings for new vintages. This is because wine merchants that have a longstanding relationship with top châteaux or estates are often able to get in large orders at the earliest price. Replacement costs for wines from good vintages are always higher.

Go to a wine supermarket like Liquor Barn or Cost Plus if you know exactly what you want to buy. If you are less certain, then go to a store that stocks less but is known for quality. There, no matter what you buy, you are likely to get more carefully chosen wines and better service. Most wine lovers who can do so shop both places. Sometimes it is worth a few dollars more to get the kind of individual attention, advice, and services (like free delivery) that smaller stores offer.

France

The world's most expensive wines are made in France, but it also produces prototypes for some of the very best moderate-priced wines. You can still drink well for $5 to $8 with the likes of Beaujolais, Muscadet, Pinot Blanc, Côtes-du-Rhône, a dollar or so more for wines like Mâcon-Villages, Saint-Véran, even quite respectable Bordeaux among the *Cru bourgeois* and certain proprietary brands.

In the southern regions of France, long known for huge quantities of mediocre wine, tremendous retrenchment is under way, with new plantings of varieties like Cabernet Sauvignon, Merlot, Syrah, and Chardonnay. Stylish new wines from regions like Provence, the Ardèche, Languedoc, and the southwest, are creating a lot of excitement. Not all of them fall within our price limit, but a good many do.

French wines traditionally have place names —region (Bordeaux), village (Sancerre), or vineyard (La Tâche, or Château Latour). The practice of naming wines for grape variety (Riesling, Chardonnay, Pinot Blanc) existed only in Alsace. In recent years French producers, noting the U.S. market for varietal wines, have enthusiastically leaped on the bandwagon with moderately priced Chardonnay, Cabernet, Merlot, and Sauvignon Blanc. It's a category to be wary of because quality varies considerably; exceptions are noted.

This chapter is arranged alphabetically by region—Bordeaux, the Loire Valley, then subdivided into the leading wines of the region. Varietal wines are treated separately.

ALSACE

Alsace is the only fine-wine region of France that makes use of varietal names. As a whole, the region produces wine of higher overall quality than any other in France. Alsace produces mostly white wines: Riesling, Gewurztraminer, Pinot Blanc, Sylvaner, Pinot Gris (also known as Tokay d'Alsace), and Muscat. What is notable is that they are dry, a surprise (even a shock sometimes) to wine drinkers used to sweet Rieslings, and Gewurz. Alsace wines age superbly—in fact, Riesling and Gewurztraminer are usually better in their third or fourth years, and they can easily last a decade if well stored.

Large shippers like Trimbach, Hugel, Leon Beyer, and Dopff & Irion established the high standards for Alsace wines, making them available at moderate prices. In the last decade individual growers like Domaine Weinbach, Zind-Humbrecht, and a few others have risen to prominence with truly remarkable Riesling,

Gewurztraminer, Muscat, and Pinot Gris. Prices
for these limited-quantity wines have also risen,
steeply in some cases. Alsace Gewurztraminer
and Pinot Gris are over $10 a bottle now. Ries-
ling and Pinot Blanc, however, remain excellent
values, particularly from the large shippers.

One fact in the consumer's favor is that Alsace wines are not as well known or understood
in the United States as other French wines, so
you may find them marked down or on special
at prices within the $10 limit. With this in mind,
some producers are included with ✳ for wines
that are just over the limit at full markup.

Gewurztraminer

The most distinctive of Alsace wines, intensely
fragrant, with sweet spicy/floral aromas that are
quite different from any other wine. Bone-dry,
it's not to everyone's taste, by any means. Alsace Gewurz cannot be compared to versions
made elsewhere, which are usually sweet. Most
of the best from Alsace now cost more than $10,
even those that aren't Reserves, thus the exclu-
sion of excellent wines from Deiss, Josmeyer,
Weinbach, and Zind-Humbrecht (though keep
an eye out for markdowns).

Age: 2–3 years, can age and improve 5–10
Price: $8–10+
Recommended Producers: Lucien Albrecht, Leon
  Beyer, La Cigogne, Dopff & Irion, Klug, J. L.
  Mader, Pierre Sparr, Trimbach ♦, Zind-Hum-
  brecht ♦
Foods: A dramatic aperitif; excellent with foie gras
  and liver pâté; rich Oriental dishes like General
  Tso's chicken and other deep-fried foods; can be
  too overpowering for lighter dishes

Pinot Blanc

Fresh, crisp, and dry, Pinot Blanc is one of the best Alsace values. In California it comes closer to Chardonnay than here, where it is more neutral in character, brisk but fruity, very appealing and quite versatile with food.

Age: 1–3 years
Price: $5–8
Recommended Producers: E. Boeckel, Leon Beyer, Clos St. Landelin, Marcel Deiss, Dopff & Irion, Hugel Cuvée des Amours, Josmeyer Mise du Printemps ✪, Klug, Gustave Lorentz, Pierre Sparr, Trimbach, A. Willm Cordon d'Alsace, Zind-Humbrecht ◆
Foods: Simply prepared fish, white meat chicken, seafood pastas, chicken or veal sausage, quiche; also excellent aperitif

Riesling

Probably the best-known Alsace wine, it is dry and steely when quite young but softens as it matures. I like Alsace Rieslings best at three to four years, when the firmness has become more supple and the wine's flowery fragrance is more apparent. Younger Rieslings have the appealing zest of green apples or citrus, with mouthwatering acidity that gets the taste buds going. Those recommended here represent excellent value.

Age: 2–4 years, but some hold easily for 4–6, and can age to 10
Price: $7–10
Recommended Producers: Adam, Lucien Albrecht, Leon Beyer, Le Cigogne, Dopff & Irion, Dopff "Au Moulin" ✳, Klug, G. Lorentz, J. L. Mader,

Pierre Sparr, Trimbach, Zind-Humbrecht Her-
renweg Turckheim ♦ ✳, Willm
Foods: Ideal with Oriental foods, including
Chinese, Thai, Vietnamese, Indian, and more
versatile than Gewürztraminer; superb with
broiled trout or sole, *coq au Riesling, choucroute*
and other sausage dishes, roast pork, ham; an excellent aperitif

Sylvaner

Dry and agreeable, quite inexpensive but too
often vapid in terms of character; not recommended in light of above values, which are
more widely available. The exceptions: Adam,
Domaine Weinbach, Trimbach.

BORDEAUX (Red)

Bordeaux enjoyed a string of superb vintages in
the 1980s, particularly 1986, 1988, and 1989.
Prices have steadily risen also. Still, it is not as
difficult as it might seem to find good, drinkable
Bordeaux for under $10. There are numerous
properties known as *petits châteaux* that offer
excellent value, the most consistent of which
are listed below.

Also included are wines from satellite areas
adjacent to the premiere districts of the Médoc,
Pomerol, Saint-Emilion, and Graves. These regions—such as Fronsac, Canon-Fronsac, Côtes
de Bourg, Côtes de Blaye, Côtes de Castillon,
Côtes de Francs—have undergone considerable
renovation and replanting in the last decade.
Several good wines from these regions are included in the long list below, but value-con-
scious consumers should be aware that new
ones continue to come along.

Listed here is a personal selection of wines that have shown consistent quality and style for several vintages. Usually blends of Merlot, Cabernet Sauvignon, and/or Cabernet Franc, these dry, firm reds emphasize fruit over depth; they have the character of fine Bordeaux but on a smaller scale, and they are ready to drink within two to five years. Note the Superbuys.

Best Bordeaux Vintages

1990	1985
1989	1983
1988	1982
1986	

Proprietary brands are listed in a separate category.

Age: 2–5 years, will go a decade in good vintages
Price: $7–10
Foods: Lamb, beef, duck, cheeses like Camembert, Port Salut, goat cheese
Recommended Châteaux (Wines with ♦ are over $10 at full markup but are frequently discounted):

Abiet (Haut-Médoc)
Beaumont (Haut-Médoc)
Bel Air (Haut-Médoc)
de Belcier ✪ (Côtes de Castillon)
Canon-Moueix ♦ (Canon-Fronsac)
Cap de Mourlin (St. Emilion) ♦
La Cardonne (Médoc)
de Carles (Fronsac)
Chantegrive ✪ (Graves)
Cissac ♦ (Haut-Médoc)
du Cros (Côtes de Castillon)
La Dauphine (Fronsac)
La Duchesse (Canon Fronsac)
du Gazin (Fronsac)
de La Grave (Bordeaux Supérieur)
de Francs (Côtes de Francs)

Fonroque ♦ (St. Emilion)

Fonplégade (St. Emilion)

Fonneuve (Première Côtes de Bordeaux)

La Fontaine (Fronsac)

La Garde (Graves)

Greysac (Haut-Médoc)

La Grolet (Côtes de Blaye)

Guirand Cheval Blanc (Côtes de Bourg)

Haut-Sociando (Côtes de Blaye)

de Juge (Premières Côtes de Bordeaux)

Lanessan ♦ (Haut-Médoc)

Larose-Trintaudon ✪ (Haut-Médoc)

Liversan (Haut-Médoc)

Livran (Médoc)

Malescasse ♦ (Haut-Médoc)

Moulin Rouge (Côtes de Castillon)

Les Moines (Médoc)

Patache d'Aux ♦ (Haut-Médoc)

Piron (Graves)

Pitray (Côtes de Castillon)

Plagnac (Médoc)

Potensac (Médoc) ♦

Puyguerrand (Côtes de Francs)

Ramage La Batisse (Médoc)

Reysson (Haut-Médoc)

Senéjac (Haut-Médoc)

Tayac ♦ (Côtes de Bourg)

La Tour de By ♦ (Médoc)

La Tour de Mons ♦ (Soussans-Margaux)

La Vieille Cure ✳ (Fronsac)

Vieux Meyney (Bordeaux)

Villars (Fronsac)

Proprietary Brands (Red)

Some excellent buys in proprietary brands have emerged in recent years. They represent some of the best bargains in red Bordeaux. Several top châteaux—Cos d'Estournel, Lynch-Bages, Ducru-Beaucaillou, among others—are producing simple but good quality, immediately drinkable reds that are excellent value.

Age: 2–4 years
Price: $5–8
Recommended Producers: Château Beau-Rivages, Château Bonnet, Jean Cordier, Fondation 1725, Lauretan, Maître d'Estournel, Mouton Cadet, Michel Lynch Rouge ✪, Château Timberlay

BORDEAUX (White, Dry)

Good inexpensive dry white Bordeaux is somewhat more plentiful than formerly, but mostly under proprietary labels, as listed below. The region Entre-Deux-Mers produces mostly dry white wines, which are gradually improving, but a great many of them are mediocre. White Bordeaux is made from Sauvignon Blanc or Sauvignon blended with Sémillon, with the tart, slightly herbacious character that makes it difficult to drink except with food. Most are intended for drinking early. My main complaint about these wines is that they still tend to be oversulphured—except for those listed below.

Age: 1–3 years
Price: $6–10
Recommended Producers: Château Bonnet, du Bordier, du Cros, Doisy-Daene, Ducla, Domaine Challon, Dourthe Frères, Fondation 1725, Château du Juge, Château Launay, l'Etoile, Maître d'Estournel, Michel Lynch, Saint-Jovian, Château de Sours, Château Thieuley.

BEAUJOLAIS

Beaujolais is actually a district within the larger
appellation of Burgundy. These popular fruity
reds, often best when lightly chilled, are made
from the Gamay grape, however, not Pinot
Noir, the grape used for red Burgundy. If you
drive from Paris to Provence and the Côte
d'Azur, the hills of Beaujolais begin to rise on
your right south of Mâcon and continue to
Lyons. Beaujolais is the quintessential quaffing
wine, one of the best light reds for summer, and
versatile with many types of food. Its charm derives from the generous and sometimes quite
intense fruit of Gamay, hinting of ripe berries
and spice. The thing to know about Beaujolais
is that there are levels of quality, ranging from
simple Beaujolais, the lightest, to Beaujolais-
Villages and then the *crus*—wines named for
the communes where the grapes are grown such
as Brouilly, Fleurie, Moulin à Vent (listed under
Crus). Beaujolais and Beaujolais-Villages are
best consumed within a year, Villages somewhat longer. The *crus* can go two years for the
lightest (Brouilly, Regnié), up to three or four
for more substantial ones (Juliénas, Morgon,
Moulin à Vent).

Beaujolais Nouveau. It is also important to
know that Beaujolais *nouveau* (literally "new
Beaujolais") is the first wine to become available after the harvest, released officially on the
third Thursday of November. Very fruity, often
highly perfumed with the scent of raspberries,
it can be a delightful quaff and should always be
lightly chilled. Originally, it served as a sort of
stopgap, light, fruity wine intended for drinking

only a few months until the year's wine *(Beaujolais de l'année)* became available in the spring. Today, half of the Beaujolais crop (excluding the *crus*) now goes into *nouveau*. Shipped all over the world, it has become a bit heavier and more intense. Most *nouveau*, however, should be consumed by March or April following the vintage. Small amounts of Beaujolais Blanc and Rosé are also made in the region.

Beaujolais. Wines labeled simply Beaujolais are the lightest of the region and not always the best value. In a ripe, sunny year like 1989, simple Beaujolais proved an excellent value, but most years Beaujolais-Villages (see) is a better buy. It is usually best when lightly chilled.

Age: Up to a year
Price: $5–7
Recommended Producers: Georges Duboeuf, Louis Jadot, Louis Latour, Louis Tête

Beaujolais Blanc

A dry white made from Chardonnay grown in the Beaujolais region, mostly the northern part west of Mâcon. Similar to Mâcon-Villages but often lighter and not often seen in the United States.

Age: 1–2 years
Price: $8–10+
Recommended Producers: Georges Duboeuf, Louis Jadot, Pierre Ferraud
Foods: Simple fish, chicken salad, cold meats, veal sausage; also a good dry aperitif

Beaujolais Nouveau

Not always the lightest in body, but certainly the fruitiest and most ephemeral of the Beaujolais. It can be delightful from Thanksgiving and through the winter. Buy it then; by April it has often lost its fresh appeal, though in some years it will hold up a few months longer. I'm appalled, however, when I see *nouveau* that is a year, two years, even *three* years old for sale in a wineshop. *Avoid* such wines at any price. *Nouveau* is best lightly chilled, which makes the fruit snappier and fresher. Also, if you pay more than $7.49 for *nouveau,* you are paying too much.

Age: 2–6 months
Price: $5–7.50
Recommended Producers: B&G, Jean Bédin, Bouchard Père et Fils, Georges Duboeuf ✪, Pierre Ferraud, Sylvain Fessy, Jaffelin, Prosper Maufoux, Mommessin, Antonin Rodet
Foods: All types of casual fare, hamburgers, chicken wings, cold meats, saucissons and other sausages, cheeses mild or savory

Beaujolais Rosé

A dry, fruity rosé made from the Beaujolais grape, Gamay. Can be delightfully fresh, crisp, and appealing but it is not often seen in the United States. Drink within a year. Best producer: Georges Duboeuf.

Beaujolais-Villages

Usually the best value in Beaujolais, fuller in body than simple Beaujolais, and fruitier. The

grapes come from about thirty villages on the
lower slopes north and west of Villefranche.
Beaujolais's fruity charm is most freely expressed in Beaujolais-Villages. The best *nouveau* is often Villages.

Age: 12–18 months
Price: $5–8
Recommended Producers: B&G, Jean Bédin, Paul
   Beaudet, René Berrod, Joseph Drouhin, Georges
   Duboeuf ✪, Pierre Ferraud, Sylvain Fessy, Louis
   Jadot, Château de Lacarelle, Maurice Des-
   combes, Prosper Maufoux, Mommessin, Joel
   Rochette, Antonin Rodet, Trenel
Foods: Same as for *nouveau*

The Crus

The term *cru* means "growth" and refers to a
classified vineyard or specially defined area, in
this case designated communes, or villages, of
Beaujolais. It is the region's highest appellation
in terms of quality. The wines have more body,
more flesh, more intense fruit, and richer texture than simple Beaujolais or Villages. There
are ten of them, and they vary somewhat in
weight and intensity. Brouilly, Côte de Brouilly,
Regnié, and Chiroubles are the lightest of the
crus in body and color, but a wonderful fruiti-
ness is their main appeal. Saint-Amour, Fleurie,
and Juliénas are deeper in color but juicy and
flavorful. Fleurie, the most popular of the *crus*,
has the most extravagant aromas of berryish
fruit with a hint of spice and roses; it is also the
most expensive, sometimes hitting $12 or $15 a
bottle. The richest and darkest of the *crus* are
Chénas, Morgon, and Moulin à Vent, the latter
occasionally almost Burgundian in character.

These wines are somewhat more age-worthy. Moulin à Vent has been known to hold well five to ten years.

Be careful when buying the *crus*. Initial mark-ups can be high, especially for Fleurie, Morgon, and Moulin à Vent. Producers like Georges Duboeuf (dubbed the "king of Beaujolais" in France) make every effort to hold prices at $10 or under, but at current exchange rates many of the *crus* have pushed beyond that. It pays to shop around for the best price because they are often marked down, but don't buy just on price. There are poor wines among the *crus* too. Stick to the recommended producers unless someone you trust touts someone else.

Age: 1–3 years, some will hold longer in good vintages; Morgon and Moulin à Vent up to 5 or more

Price: $7.50–10+

Recommended Producers: Jean Bédin, Château de la Chaize (Brouilly), Joseph Drouhin, Georges Duboeuf ☉, Pierre Ferraud, Sylvain Fessy, Jacky Janodet ♦, Louis Jadot, Prosper Maufoux, Mommessin, Joel Rochette, Trenel ♦

Foods: Chicken, sausages, liver and kidney, roast pork, goat cheese, semisoft cheeses, blues

BURGUNDY (White)

While the great whites from the Côte d'Or are beyond the scope of this book, there are excellent buys in wines from the Mâconnais region and, very occasionally, the Côte Chalonnais (Rully and Montagny). White wines from any Burgundy appellation are made from Chardonnay, though Aligoté is a lesser white grape that is also grown in parts of the region.

Chardonnay produces the greatest of the world's dry white wines, and some of the most expensive. But Chardonnay also performs at lesser levels, yielding stylish, vibrant, and very appealing wines that offer superb value. They are wines that drink best in one to three years. Their clean, crisp flavors, simpler and more neutral than the bigger, more expensive whites of the Côte d'Or (Meursault, Chablis, the Montrachets), can handle a variety of foods.

Aligoté

Aligoté is a white grape that runs a distant second to Chardonnay in Burgundy. It is a dry, medium-bodied white, fruity but fairly neutral in character. Traditionally it was the wine used in the popular aperitif Kir, which consists of a few drops of *crème de cassis* and dry white wine. Aligoté is still used for the Kir in Burgundy, though today the wine may well be Mâcon-Villages. Young, well-balanced Aligoté can be quite pleasant, and a decent buy, and has recently become more widely available in the United States.

Age: 1–2 years
Price: $9–10
Recommended Producers: Boillot, Domaine Roche-beau, Faiveley La Paulée, Louis Jadot, Louis La-tour, Prosper Maufoux, Noirot, P. Morey ♦, M. Rollin
Foods: Light fish, chicken, steamed vegetables; good aperitif, especially with cassis (Kir)

Bourgogne Blanc

Always Chardonnay and now often labeled as such. The wines can come from anywhere in Burgundy, so do not always show well-defined or distinctive character. From some producers, however, it is quite good, dry, and full-bodied, with the firm, slightly steely fruit of simple Burgundian Chardonnay. Aged briefly in oak, sometimes not at all. If you find it for $10 from a good producer, you get great value. Prices for Bourgogne Blanc have risen, however, and if you want to stay at $10 or less, check out discount stores, or look for Saint-Véran.

Age: 1–3 years, some will go 4 or 5
Price: $8–10+
Recommended Producers: Boisson-Morey, Hubert Bouzereau, Chartron & Trebuchet ◆, Joseph Drouhin, P. Javillier ◆, Louis Latour, Henri Meurgey, J. Moreau Chardonnay, J. Pascal
Foods: Fish, chicken breast, shellfish; aperitif or Kir

Bourgogne Rouge

Made entirely from pinot noir, wines labeled Bourgogne Rouge are even scarcer than Bourgogne Blanc. A lot more is produced than ever makes it to the United States, among them some quite expensive (Leroy, $17). Good ones are like lesser Burgundies, with appealing Pinot Noir fruit, simple and forthright, with less tannin and body, though some Bourgogne can be rather gutsy. Poor ones can be thin, hard, and lacking in charm. Bourgogne Passe-tous-grains, more rarely seen, is a fruity blend of Pinot Noir and Gamay.

Age: 2–5 years
Price: $8–10+
Recommended Producers: Pierre Bourée ♦, Coche Debord, De Courcel, André Delorme, Joseph Drouhin, Dubreuil-Fontaine, J. Faiveley, Jayer-Gilles ✳, H. Lamy, Lupe-Cholet, J. Monnier, Domaine Tallmard, du Vieux St. Sorlin, Comte de Bailly
Foods: Duck, coq au vin, liver and kidney, veal, goat cheese

Mâcon-Villages (also known as Mâcon Blanc, Mâcon Clessé, Mâcon Ige, Mâcon-Lugny, Mâcon-Viré)

The best-known and most widely available white Burgundy, from a large region of vineyards near the town of Mâcon. Pinot Noir and Gamay are also grown here, but the region is known mostly for Mâcon Blanc. Fresh, crisp, very dry, sometimes to the point of seeming austere, it is made entirely from Chardonnay. Most wines are not aged in oak, giving them a simple fruit character. Mâcon from good, reputable producers is an excellent value, and there are many, though numerous mediocre ones exist as well. Prices for some wines have inched beyond $10, but there are plenty of good buys for that or less.

Age: 1–2 years, can go 3
Price: $7–10+
Recommended Producers: André Bonhomme, Collin & Bourisset, Domaine Fichet, Domaine Perrin, Domaine Prieuré, Domaine des Roches, Domaine de Rochebin, Joseph Drouhin, Georges Duboeuf ○, Louis Jadot, Louis Latour, Cave des Lugny Les Charmes, Prosper Maufoux, Michel

Nathan, Domaine Tallmard, Domaine Teissédre,
Caves de Viré Le Grand Cheneau
Foods: Simply prepared fish, shrimp, scallops,
chicken breast, cold roast chicken or turkey,
chicken salad, quiche; also a good aperitif, makes
an excellent Kir

Saint-Véran ✪

This appellation, also in the Mâconnais region,
is a cut above Mâcon-Villages in character and
body and an excellent alternative to Pouilly-
Fuissé, which are now well beyond $10. Some
Saint-Véran also cost a few dollars more, but
excellent ones can be found for $10, sometimes
less, especially at discount stores. Saint-Véran
is often given a few months in oak, which gives
it an extra degree of richness and complexity.

Age: 2–4 years
Price: $8–10
Recommended Producers: Paul Beaudet, Cave de
Lugny Les Monts, Domaine Colombiers, Do-
maine Laroche, T. Guerin, Georges Duboeuf ✪,
Jean-Claude Boisset, Louis Jadot, Prosper Mau-
foux, Michel Nathan, Les Trois Pêcheurs, J. J.
Vincent
Foods: Richer fish preparations, shellfish, fish or
chicken in cream sauce, seafood pastas, goat
cheese

LANGUEDOC-ROUSILLON
AND THE SOUTHWEST

This sprawling region in southern France, often
referred to as the Midi, teems with vineyards
that for years produced mostly plonk. Buckets
of plonk are still produced here, but enterpris-

ing producers have replanted many vineyards to better varieties (Cabernet, Merlot, Syrah, Chardonnay) and have modernized production. Some very appealing red wines have begun to surface in parts of the Languedoc, particularly within appellations like Côtes de Rousillon, Gard, Aude, Corbières and Minervois, as well as stylish nonappellation wines from these areas, mostly varietal wines labeled Cabernet Sauvignon, Merlot, and Chardonnay.

Some of these wines have been so highly praised that prices have streaked well beyond $10. Frankly I question whether in some cases they are worth it. Wines that seemed remarkable values when they were unknown and sold for $8 or $10 do not always seem a great value at $16 or $18. Some terrific values for $7 to $10 remain, however. Best buys within our price range are listed below, but it is worth noting that new properties are coming on line; so be on the lookout for new discoveries.

In terms of age, styles vary. A Corbières like Domaine de Fontsainte (see Corbières) is quite drinkable when you buy it, though substantial enough to age four or five years. A denser, more tannic red like Château de Campuget, however, needs a good two or three years to become so. Check it out with your wine merchant; if he knows enough to stock these wines, he should be able to advise you about drinkability.

Age: 2–8 years, depending on the wine
Price: $7–10
Recommended Producers: **Domaine Bouscasse Madiran, Domaine du Bas Deffens, Domaine de la Bousquette, Daniel Bessière, Faugères Alquier, Château Calabre, Château Grinou, Château de Gourgazaud, Château de Jau, Château Etang des**

Colombes, Domaine de La Roque, Domaines du Bas Geffens, Domaine Doña Baisses, La Source-ltérault, Domaine de Pouy Ugni Blanc ✪, Domaine Les Jouglas, Domaine de Rieux, Domaine Ste.-Eulalie, Alain Junguenet, Château Montus Madiran, Château Paraza, Patrimoine, Rèserve St. Martin ✪, Château Rouquette Sur Mer, St. Chinian, Sarda-Mallet

Cahors

A sound, balanced red made mostly from Malbec blended with Tannat and Merlot or Cabernet Sauvignon. The region is east of Bordeaux, and the wines are somewhat similar but lighter. The best have good structure, a good smack of tannin that allows them to age several years. Cahors is a terrific value—not a lot is available in the United States, but most of what does come in is from the better producers. As its popularity and value are recognized, prices are rising, but good ones can be had for $10, or less.

Age: 2–6 years, can go 8–10
Price: $8–10
Recommended Producers: Château de Chambert, Clos de Gamot, Clos Triguedina, Domaine de Bovila, Domaine de Haute-Serre, Moulin de la Grezette ✪, Château Pech de Jammes ♦, Château de Peyros, Domaine de Quattre, La Tour de Vayrols
Foods: Lamb, beef, veal, meat stews, mellow cheeses like Mimolette, Port Salut

Corbières

The region of Corbières has exploded in new or replanted vineyards in recent years. Rhône varieties like Syrah, Mourvèdre, Carignan, and

Grenache produce some of the sturdiest, most attractive reds, such as Domaine Fontsainte. Many of the same varieties are used for brisk, dry Corbières rosé. Some of the whites are also appealing, more so in fact than the majority of Rhône whites of similar price levels. The whites are usually blends of Grenache Blanc, Ugni Blanc, and Bourboulenc, with varying amounts of Chardonnay or Sauvignon Blanc. They are simple and dry but fresh when very young, and quite versatile with food. New labels are rapidly surfacing, and worth inquiring about from your wine merchant.

Age: 1–2 years for Corbières blanc and rosé, 2–4 for rouge, can hold for 5–8
Price: $5–10
Recommended Producers: Château Beauregard, Jean Berail Roque, Clos Villemajou, Domaine Fontsainte "Reserve la Demoiselle ✪," Château Saint Auriol, Domaine Serres Mazard, Château La Voulte Gasparets
Foods: Hearty meats and cheeses with reds; ham, smoked meats, and grilled vegetables with rosé; light fish, chicken and pasta with whites

---

LOIRE VALLEY

The Loire Valley is a scant two hours by autoroute from Paris. The Loire River runs some six hundred miles from the center of France to the Atlantic. This picturesque region, with its historic châteaux, charming towns, and pastoral countryside, is home to several of France's best-known wines, including Muscadet, Sancerre, Chinon, and Vouvray. Most are white or rosé, except for Chinon, Bourgueil, and a soupçon of Sancerre Rouge.

The top appellations of Sancerre, Pouilly-Fumé and Savennières, all dry whites, have escalated in price in recent years; there are a few exceptions noted. Muscadet, however, remains one of the great French wine values, especially in recent vintages, which have been very good to excellent. The wines of the Loire are treated alphabetically according to appellation.

Anjou

In this country most people think of sweetish rosés when they hear of the region Anjou. In fact, many of the best Anjou wines are dry whites, rosés, and supple red wines that nicely suit local cuisine. Anjou rouge, made from Cabernet Franc or Gamay, is a gently-structured red that is best chilled, which makes it suitable for light meats, hearty pastas, or semisoft cheeses. Recommended: Domaine Baumard Logis de Giraudière, about $8.

Rosés are made all over the Loire and are almost invariably dry, but sweetened for export. Too bad. The dry ones are light-bodied, fruity, and refreshing, wonderful lunch and picnic wines when you are traveling through the valley. Cabernet d'Anjou seems to have a little more dash and character than Rosé d'Anjou and is less cloyingly sweet. Recommended: Domaine de la Motte, Sauvion et Fils, $5–6.

Bourgueil

This is one of the better reds produced in the Loire, not very well known in the United States but very popular in Paris bistros and wine bars. Produced from Cabernet Franc, it has lively fruit hinting of berries and herbs. Good ones are soft and drinkable early, but some have the depth to age five or six years. Some of the best wines are labeled St. Nicholas de Bourgeuil.

Age: 2–4 years, can go 5 or 6
Price: $8–10
Recommended Producers: Audebert, Cognard, Domaine de la Gennetière, Domaine du Grand Clos, Les Cloitres, Marcel Martin, Domaine Nicolas Jamet
Foods: Light meats and game birds, goat cheese

Chinon

Chinon and Bourgeuil are often mentioned in the same breath. Both are made from Cabernet Franc, but Chinon is somewhat more vivid in fruit and flavor—and generally more expensive. Top producers like Joguet and Druet make impressive wines that can age a decade (they cost $17 to $20). Lighter, decent Chinon can be found, such as Domaine Morin, O. Raffault, Colombier, Marcel Martin, or Domaine de la Chenétrie, but once you've tasted a flashier one, they may not satisfy. The lighter ones benefit from light chilling. Try discount shops where you may find Couly-Dutheil, for instance, for $10 or $11.

Ménétou-Salon

The red, white, and rosé wines of this appellation are some of the Loire's most charming. Very few are available in this country, unfortunately, and those that are tend to be overpriced. In the Loire Valley they are not expensive, with many well under $10 a bottle. The whites, made from Sauvignon Blanc, can be an alternative to the more expensive Sancerre and Pouilly-Fumé. The rosés are dry and light-bodied, the reds fruity and smooth. Few labels are here as yet, but perhaps we will see more in the future.

Age: 1–2 years, 2–4 for reds
Price: $8–10
Recommended Producers: Domaine Chatenoy, Le Brun St. Ceols
Foods: Roast chicken, lamb, or quail with red; fish, seafood, chicken breast with white; pork, ham, smoked duck, or turkey with rosé; goat cheese with all three.

Muscadet ✪

This crisp, snappy dry white offers terrific value. It's a great summer wine, superb with fresh oysters the rest of the year. It comes from the region closest to the Atlantic, and is a versatile match with all sorts of seafood. The best Muscadet comes from the heart of the region known as Sèvre et Maine. The overall quality of Muscadet is higher than it used to be, a result of keen competition among the top producers. It is best consumed within two years of the vintage, when the fruit is fresh and sharp as an ocean breeze.

Age: 1–2 years, maybe 3
Price: $5–8
Recommended Producers: Barré Frères, A. Bregeon, Château du Cléray, Château La Nöe, Château de la Rogotière, Domaine de l'Hyvernière, Les Haut Bretonnières, Marquis de Goulaine, Marcel Martin, Louis Metaireau, Domaine de la Quilla, Sauvion et Fils ✪

Quincy

Barely known in the United States, this crisp white made from Sauvignon Blanc is a good alternative to the more expensive wines from this grape, Sancerre and Pouilly-Fumé. While it lacks their character and finesse, it is fresh, lively, and attractive.

Age: 1–2 years
Price: $7–9
Recommended Producers: Sauvion et Fils
Foods: Grilled or broiled fish, goat cheese

Sancerre

This distinctive white, made from Sauvignon Blanc, is one of my favorites from the Loire. Its crisp, tart fruit has its own *goût de terroir,* reminiscent of herbs, new-mown grass, and citrus with an appealing, mineral-like flavor. Scintillatingly dry, it is one of those wines that stir up the taste buds and whet the appetite. Prices, alas, have risen considerably as its popularity has increased. To find good Sancerre within our price limit, you'll have to search in discount stores or watch for specials.

Age: 2–3 years
Price: $9–10+ *(sales or specials)*
Recommended Producers: Archambault Clos de la Perrière ♦, Château de Sancerre, Comte Lafond, Cordier Le Chaillou, Langlois ♦, Daniel Millet ♦, Roger Neveu, Domaine du Sarry, Château Thauvenay
Foods: Superb with goat cheese from the Loire; also fine with fish and seafood, *boudin blanc,* pâté

Savennières

The most interesting and complex dry white made from Chenin Blanc. Savennières is one of the Loire's finest whites and usually costs more than $10. Structured to age, which it can do for several years, it is prized by connoisseurs who understand its uniqueness. Even lesser ones are pleasant to drink, however, fruity, fragrant, dry, medium-bodied but with a certain richness. The top property, Coulée de Serrant, costs $30; others can be found for less at discount stores.

Age: 2–5 years, best can go 8 or 10
Price: $8–10+
Recommended Producers: Château de Chambousseau, Clos du Papillon ♦, Roche aux Moines ♦
Foods: Fish such as sea bass, red snapper, or swordfish, sautéed chicken, country pâté

Vouvray

Vouvray, made in the Touraine region from Chenin Blanc, is not easy to buy because you are rarely sure of what you are getting, especially at lower prices. Is it sweet or dry, or off-dry? If it is sweet, the label usually says Demi-sec. These can be wonderful wines and they last for years, but the finest are rare and expensive. Dry Vouvray is rarely labeled Sec—also rarely is it truly dry. When it is well balanced, a hint of sweetness adds richness and complexity and the wine is charming. Some Vouvrays, however, lack finesse and can be oversulphured.

Age: 2–4 years for Vouvray Sec, considerably longer for Demi-sec
Price: $8–10+
Recommended Producers: Marc Brédif, D. Champolou, Château de Moncontour, Château de

Montfort, Clos Naudin, Kermit Lynch, Monmousseau, Prince Poniatowski ♦
Foods: Dry Vouvray with smoked trout, *rillette,*
liver, or country pâté, rabbit stew; Vouvray
Demi-sec is a dessert wine, best on its own or
with light cakes or cookies

PROVENCE

The south of France is churning. This large region stretches from the hills of Provence to the
Midi. Together the two regions produce the
bulk of France's so-called "country" wines and
vins de table. The new generation of winegrow-
ers is transforming this sprawling landscape,
planting new grape varieties (*cépages* in
French), and establishing new quality standards. Many of the reds have vivid fruit and
vigorous, muscular structure—rustic, spicy,
earthy, and appealing. The whites are less exciting, but cleaner, fresher, zestier than they used
to be; some are quite charming, in fact.

Some of the most dynamic wines come from
Provence; many of the hot ones (Bandols such
as Domaine Tempier, Ott, Pibarnou) have
jumped in price well beyond $10 a bottle. While
in some instances the steeper price tag is de-
served, in others it is highly presumptuous, particularly for whites and rosés. Seekers of
genuine value, however, such as Kermit Lynch
and Robert Kacher, have turned up some rich
and chewy little marvels that are excellent
value. These names on a bottle mean the wine
is always worth checking out.

Age: Ready to drink, though some reds can age 4–8
years or more
Price: $5–10

Recommended Producers: **Domaine La Moutête,
Domaine Gavoty, Domaine de la Gautier, Domaine La Rosière, Domaine Richeaume Rouge
and *Rosé*, Mas de Cadenet Rouge and Blanc ✪,
Mas de Gourgonnier ✪, Mas de la Rouvière**

THE RHÔNE VALLEY

The Côtes-du-Rhône occupies a long, narrow
corridor south of Lyons to Avignon. With vineyards situated either side of the Rhône River,
the 120-mile valley produces some of France's
greatest wines, especially grand, robust reds
like Hermitage, Côte Rotie, and Châteauneuf-
du-Pape—all of which are fairly grand in price
too. Fortunately the Rhône also abounds in
good, drinkable wines at moderate prices—Gigondas, Crozes-Hermitage, Vacqueyras. For casual occasions, or an everyday red, it's hard to
beat good Côtes-du-Rhône or its little brother,
Côtes du Ventoux. These large appellations in
the southern part of the Rhône make up more
than 75 percent of total production, over 20 million cases annually. Most is quite ordinary, even
mediocre, but exceedingly good ones exist if you
know what to look for.

The best values in the Rhône are red. While
the region makes very fine expensive whites
(Condrieu, Hermitage Blanc, the sweet Muscat
Beaumes de Venise), the less expensive whites
are generally disappointing, coarse in flavor,
and often lacking in freshness. The few exceptions are noted where appropriate. Tavel and
other rosés are covered in the Rosé section
(see).

Côtes-du-Rhône

The general appellation covers light-bodied, fruity reds made from several grape varieties grown in the southern Rhône as well as the noble red grape of the northern Rhône, Syrah. Good Côtes-du-Rhône has round, appealing, berryish fruit. The best ones, such as those from E. Guigal, Domaine Ste.-Anne, Jaboulet, and others, are more intense, with peppery accents and very meaty flavors. Several such wines constitute Superbuys.

Age: 2–3 years, 4–6 for the best
Price: $6–9
Recommended Producers: Château d'Aigueville, Château de Tours, Domaine Brusset, Domaine Durieu Clos de Cazeaux, Cru de Coudelet ♦, Domaine Ste.-Anne ✪ (also the Blanc), Domaine de la Guizharde, Domaine de la Jasse, Domaine Santa Duc, Délas Frère, E. Guigal ✪, Les Gouberts ✪, Jaboulet ✪, Kermit Lynch ✪, Michel Courtial, Domaines de Mont-Redon, Angustin Peyrouse, Domaine St. Gayan, Saint-Estève (also the Blanc), Vidal-Fleury, Vieux Chênes
Foods: Highly versatile with casual foods, from hamburgers to barbecued meat, roast chicken, smoked turkey or duck, sausages, cheese and cheese dishes, goat cheese

Côtes du Ventoux

This is a lighter version of Côtes-du-Rhône, sometimes too light to be much good. The exceptions, as noted, are punchier, with more fruit and style and can really be a super value, especially at discount stores where they go for as little as $3.99.

Age: 1–3 years
Price: $5–7.50
Recommended Producers: Chapoutier, Jaboulet, La
   Vieille Ferme ✪, Vidal-Fleury

Crozes-Hermitage

This sturdy red from the northern Rhône is
made from Syrah grown in areas surrounding
the great hill of Hermitage. It is similar to Hermitage, but smaller in scale and less complex—
with one exception, Jaboulet's Domaine de
Thalabert, which in some vintages comes remarkably close to fine Hermitage. At full
markup it costs around $13, but frequently can
be found on special or at discounters for under
$10, making it a Superbuy. Crozes-Hermitage
can be thin and harsh in lesser vintages, though
more consistent from the better producers.

Age: 3–5 years, the best can age well for 8–10 or
   longer
Price: $9–10+
Recommended Producers: Delas Frères, Domaine
   de Thalabert (Jaboulet) ✳, M. Feneton, Jaboulet,
   Michel Courtial, Moillard, Augustin Peyrouse,
   Domaine Pradelle, Vidal-Fleury

Gigondas

This chewy, meaty red from the southern Rhône
has become more popular in recent years. Some
Gigondas is very intense and tannic in its early
years, but mellows down with two to four years
of aging. A few good ones can be found for $10
or less, others only on special or at discounters.
Sturdy and robust, it's worth searching out.

Age: 3–5 years, can age
Price: $8–10+
Recommended Producers: Clos des Cazeaux, Domaine du Gour du Chaule, Grand Montmirail, E. Guigal, Prosper Maufoux, Jaboulet, Domaine Raspail, Château du Trignon ♦
Foods: Beef, game, meat stews, cassoulet, goat cheese

Vacqueyras

The vineyards near the town of Vacqueyras in the southern Rhône produce a somewhat more meatier version of Côtes-du-Rhône and are entitled to use the appellation Côtes-du-Rhône-Villages. The fruit is more intense, the wines coarser and more tannic. Not necessarily a better buy than Côtes-du-Rhône, however, except as noted.

Age: 3–5 years
Price: $8–10
Recommended Producers: Cuvée St. Roch, Domaine de Couroulou, Dussen, Jaboulet
Foods: Meat stews, cassoulet, savory cheeses

Rhône

Other appellations are producing rich, muscular reds such as Cairanne, Côtes du Luberon, Lirac, while some (Côteaux du Tricastin, Sablet) produce more supple ones. Few of these appellations are well represented in the United States as yet, but they are beginning to see wider distribution.

Age: 2–5 years
Price: $6–10

Recommended Producers: La Bouverie, Château de Campuget (Costières de Nimes), Château Val de Joanis Rouge ✪ et Blanc (Côtes du Luberon), Château de Mille (Luberon), Domaine Les Goubert Sablet Blanc and Rouge, Domaine La Rosière Syrah, Château du Trignon Sablet and Rasteau

ROSÉS

France produces tremendous quantities of rosé wines, some dry, some sweet. A lot of it is quite mediocre, including much of the well-known sweet rosés from the Loire Valley labeled Rosé d'Anjou, and even some interpretations of the country's best-known rosé, Tavel. Tavel has long been considered France's best rosé, but this is no longer true. Today it stands in the shadow of livelier, more vibrant rosés like Joguet's Chinon Rosé, Duboeuf's Beaujolais Rosé, and the dry rosés of Burgundy. These are sometimes labeled *vin gris*—*gris* actually translates as "gray" but really means a pale coral or flesh color. Since there is so much variation in quality, the rosés recommended here are from various parts of France—the name of the producer is more important than the region. Some of the currently touted rosés, especially those from recently discovered properties in Provence, have leaped to what I consider unconscionable prices. Sixteen dollars for a simple dry rosé? Come on, that's for the "let-them-eat-cake" crowd. There are equally good ones for considerably less.

Age: 1–2 years
Price: $6–10+
Recommended Producers: Château d'Aqueria

Tavel, Domaine Bart Marsannay, Château
Beaupré Minervois, Domaine Bruno Clair Marsannay ✪, Georges Duboeuf Beaujolais, Fontsainte Gris de Gris, Domaine Gavoty Bandol,
Joguet Chinon, Domaine La Moutête, Domaine
de la Morderée Tavel, Mugner Bourgogne, Olga
Raffau Chinon, Sauvion d'Anjou, Château Ville-
rambeau Julien Minervois, A. de Villaine Bourgogne ♦

VARIETAL WINES

Except for Alsace, French wines with distinctive
character, whether expensive or modest in
price, are usually labeled with regional or vineyard names. New development in several regions—such as the Haut-Poitou of the Loire,
Provence, Languedoc-Rousillon, and several
districts in Bordeaux—has resulted in what is
building into a category all its own: varietals.
These are wines made predominantly from a
single grape variety, which appears on the label.
Those most frequently seen are Chardonnay
and Sauvignon Blanc for white wines, Cabernet
Sauvignon, Merlot, Pinot Noir, and Syrah for
reds. This category is growing fast. Several producers of *vin de table,* the nonvintage magnums
appearing under labels like Patriarche, René
Junot, Partager, etc., have begun bottling varietals. Some are quite decent, others barely a cut
above the innocuous *vins de table.*

The new varietals are not to be confused with
regional varietals like the Bourgogne Blanc
(Chardonnay) and Rouge (Pinot Noir), which
have something of the distinctive character of
their region. The newer wines are rather neutral in most cases, the best of them clean, well

balanced, tasting of the grape that produces them. As yet, there are not a great many to recommend, and the good from the mediocre are still in the process of sorting themselves out. It is definitely a category to watch.

Age: 1–2 years for whites; 2–4 for reds
Price: $4.50–8
Recommended Producers: Baron Briare (Sauvignon Blanc), Barton & Guestier, Chantovent, Michel Cravate, Domaine La Source-Herault, J. Drouhin, Georges Duboeuf, Fortant, J. Moreau, L. Jadot, René Junot, Domaine de Montmarin Langlois Château, Louis Latour, Domaine La Rosière, Domaine Ravel, Prosper Maufoux, Christian Moueix (Merlot), J. & P. Moueix, Place d'Argent, Domaine de Pouy, Regnard, Domaine Richeaume, Domaine de Rivoire, Domaine de Tuilerie, Val d'Orbieu Vallion

SUPERBUYS / FRANCE

Whites
Pinot Blanc, Alsace (Trimbach, Josmeyer, Beyer) $6–9
Château Bonnet, Bordeaux, $7.75
Domaine de Pouy, $5.99
Maître d'Estournel, Bordeaux, $6.99
Georges Duboeuf Mâcon-Village, Burgundy, $6.99
Mâcon-Lugny, Les Charmes, Burgundy, $7–8
Reserve St. Martin Blanc de Blancs, $4
Sauvion et Fils Muscadet, $6–7
Les Goubert Sablet Blanc, Rhône, $7.99

Reds
Château de Belcier, Bordeaux, $7
Château Larose Trintaudon, Bordeaux, $8.99
Michel Lynch Rouge, Bordeaux, $5.99–7

Georges Duboeuf Beaujolais (Nouveau, Villages, Regnié), $6–8

Château du Campuget, Rhône, $7.99–8.99

Domaine de Fontsainte, Corbières, $8.99

Mas de Gourgonnier, Provence, $7.50

Jaboulet La Table du Roy, Rhône, $4.50

Côte-du-Rhône Rouge (Domaine Ste.-Anne, Guigal, Jaboulet, $6–8.99)

La Vieille Ferme Rouge, Rhône, $6–7.50

Domaine de Thalabert Crozes-Hermitage, Rhône red, $9–10 ✳

Château Val de Joanis Rouge, Rhône red, $6.99

Moulin de la Grezette, Cahors, $8–9

Rosé

Bruno Clair Marsanny, $8.99

Château Rouquette Sur Mer, $8.99

Italy

Italy is a brimming vat of wine, the world's largest producer. There are nearly 2 million vineyards in Italy producing over 7 million liters of wine. Only about 12 percent of it, however, comes under the appellation laws known as *Denominazione d'origine controllata* (DOC), which comprises most of what we import to this country—in other words, we get the best.

American wine consumers used to Italian wine bargains—remember the days of $9 Barolo (*good* ones!), $7 Chianti Riserva, and $4 Pinot Grigio?—are having a rough time adjusting to double-digit prices. Those days are gone; prices for each of those wines have doubled, even tripled. One can take solace in the fact, however, that the increased global demand for good wine has forced Italian winemakers into a greater commitment to quality. This can be seen not only with the new, innovative wines that began to appear in the eighties, but with traditional types as well. Orvieto, for example, a rather ordinary, often mediocre white wine from the hill town of Umbria, has never been better than in vintages of the late eighties and early nineties—fresh, crisp, dry—all one could want in a simple, inexpensive white wine for everyday or casual occasions.

The DOC laws cover nearly five hundred different styles of Italian wine. Instituted in 1963, DOC helped raise standards for winegrowing all over Italy and brought the wines into the main arena of international recognition. If the DOC designation on a wine is somewhat less important now, it is because the law has done its work over the past two decades to give Italian winemakers a common aim: making quality wines and seeing it pay off. Today, in fact, some of the country's best wines are non-DOC—proprietary blends like Tignanello, Sammarco, La Pergola Torte, Montesodi, and dozens of others that are among Italy's most expensive wines.

For our purposes here, with our $10-a-bottle limit, we must stick to the affordable best. The list necessarily excludes some of Italy's most famous wine names, like Barolo, Barbaresco, Brunello di Montalcino, Taurasi, Arneis, and the growing host of proprietary wines like those mentioned above—they cost well upward of $15 a bottle.

Fortunately there is enough good, flavorful wine at more modest prices that those who want to enjoy Italian wines for everyday or casual occasions needn't suffer. You have to know the right producers, though. There are probably twenty-five or more Pinot Grigios available in the United States; quality varies considerably, and perhaps a dozen are worth the price—you can get burned with lousy wines or by overpaying. It's wise to stick to the names recommended here, unless your wine merchant has discovered a "find" that he personally recommends.

WHITE WINES

Italy has long been known for exceptional red wines, but whites, for the most part, were traditionally modest and simple at best, bobbing along in oceans of quite ordinary, even mediocre, wines. Italy's top whites, like Gavi di Gavi, Fiano di Avellino, and Arneis, can be interesting and quite good, but are often wildly overpriced. Tasting them makes you wonder what you are paying for. In fact, restaurant wine lists account for most of the sales in this country.

Trebbiano is the most widely grown white variety, producing most of the white wines of central Italy (Toscano Bianco, Galestro of Tuscany, Orvieto and Torgiano of Umbria, Frascati and Trebbiano di Aprilia of Latium). Some of these are rather fragile wines, often better on the spot than when they arrive on these shores. Many of them are flash-pasteurized for stabilization, which certainly doesn't add to the quality but does preserve a modicum of fruit. A few of the better ones are included here.

Bianco di Custoza

A clean dry white from the Veneto, southwest of Verona, very similar in fruit character (blended from the same white grapes) to Soave, sometimes superior. Limited distribution.

Age: 12–18 months
Price: $6–7
Recommended Producers: La Columbaia, Lamberti,
  Santa Sofia, Tommasi, Zenato
Foods: Shellfish, boiled or grilled, seafood pasta, ri-
  sotto

Bianco di Toscana

Trebbiano was traditionally the grape used for
Tuscan whites that were mild in flavor and character. Quality producers, however, have reduced yields to get more fruit intensity (as in
Coltibuono Bianco) or added better grapes such
as Pinot Bianco, Sauvignon Blanc, and Chardonnay to the blend. Good ones have appealing
fruit and bracing acidity that makes them excellent food wines.

Age: 1–2 years
Price: $7–10
Recommended Producers: Altesino, Antinori, Badia
  a Coltibuono ✪, Barbi, Brolio, Casa Francesco,
  Castellare, Castello di Volpaia, Dievole, Frescobaldi, Gabbiano, Podere Il Palazzino, Terre Tos-
  cane, Villa Cilnia Poggio Garbato, Vinattieri ◆
Foods: Antipasti; seafood pastas, pasta primavera,
  pasta with mushrooms; fish and shellfish; white
  meat chicken; prosciutto

Breganze di Breganze

This unusual proprietary white is one of the
best values from Fausto Maculan, a top producer in the Veneto. Crisp, dry, lively citrus flavors make it versatile with food. Chardonnay
gives it character.

Age: 1–2 years
Price: $8–10
Sole Producer: Fausto Maculan

Chardonnay

Chardonnay on the label is a guaranteed sale these days, no matter what the price tag. Italian Chardonnay remains one of the bargain whites in Italy in the $8–10 range. Cheaper ones are mostly from large producers whose wines have little character and therefore are *not* good buys. The better ones are dry, medium-bodied, with brisk fruit flavors. They get little or no oak aging and are quite versatile with food, more so than weightier Chardonnays, which can be overpowering for all but the richest dishes. Don't be shocked to find increasingly expensive Chardonnays coming out of Italy, especially oak-aged versions from Tuscany, Umbria, and the Piedmont. These wines, aiming at styles similar to white Burgundy and California Chardonnay, are a different breed and expensive (*and*, might I add, sometimes overpriced!).

Age: Best at 1–2 years but may go 3 or 4 from superior vintages like 1989, 1990
Price: $7–12
Recommended Producers: Boscaini, J. Brigl, Batasiolo ♦, Il Cardo, Castel San Valentino, Collavini, Fantinel, Fratelli Pighin, Castelcosa, Gaierhof, Kettmeir, Lageder, Leone de Castris, di Lozzolo, Lungarotti, Maso Poli, Nozzole Le Brunicche, Pierpaolo, Plozner ✪, Pojer & Sandri ♦, Ruffino Libaio ✪, San Felice, Istituto San Michele ✪, Santa Margherita ♦, J. Tiefenbrunner ✪, Tommasi Rafael, Villanova, Roberto Zeni ♦
Foods: Seafood pastas, risotto, shellfish, chicken breast, rabbit; also a serviceable aperitif

Frascati

Mostly light and nondescript, but dry and sometimes attractively fruity, especially those labeled *Superiore*. Not strongly recommended
since other Italian whites offer better value.

Age: 1–2 years
Price: $5–8
Recommended Producers: Centanni, Colli di Ca-
tone, Colli di Tuscolo, Fontana Candida, Pallavi-
cini
Foods: Antipasti, seafood salads, especially mussels

Galestro

Made from the white grapes of the Chianti region (Trebbiano, Pinot Bianco, Malvasia), this
brisk, light-bodied wine is also light on flavor,
too much so much of the time, and it can be
bitingly crisp. The better ones have a lively zest
that is appealing. The fruit does not hold much
beyond the first year, so beware of anything
older.

Age: 8–12 months
Price: $6–8
Recommended Producers: Antinori, Frescobaldi,
Gabbiano, Ruffino, La Chiantigiana, Rocca della
Macie, San Felice
Foods: Antipasti; also makes a good wine spritzer

Gavi

The Piedmont's best-known white wine, made
from the Cortese di Gavi grape. Well-made
Gavi is dry and medium-bodied, with lively fruit
and fresh aromas; the fruit is fairly delicate in
young wines, but flavors deepen after a couple

of years in bottle. Considered one of the top Italian whites for fish and seafood, but prices for the best ones have jumped to $15 and more; a few good ones are still available for less.

Age: 1–2 years, though some will age nicely for 2–3
Price: $8.50–10 +
Recommended Producers: Nicola Bergaglio, Bolla, Contratto, Flavio, Foro, il Cardo, Marchesi di Barolo ♦, Massone ♦, Monfrino, Villa Banfi Principessa ♦
Foods: Fish and seafood dishes, pasta with white truffles

Lacryma Christi del Vesuvio

Produced on the volcanic slopes of Vesuvius, Lacryma Christi (whose name means "tear of Christ") has long been a popular wine in and around Naples. It is simple dry white with no pretensions, but the leading estate in the region, Mastroberardino, makes something more of it than that in a crisp, attractive version, but still rather overpriced at $10 a bottle.

Age: 1–2 years
Price: $6.50–10 +
Recommended Producers: Saviano, Mastroberardino (if you feel it's worth $10)
Foods: Pasta with squid, mussels, or marinara sauce; chicken cacciatore

Lugana

A delicate white from Lombardy from a DOC region that extends into the Veneto. Not widely available in the United States, light-bodied Lugana can be fresh and charming from good producers but is sometimes dull and lacking in flavor by the time it gets here. It's at its best locally.

Age: 1 year; good ones gain in flavor up to 2 or 3
Price: $7
Recommended Producers: Lamberti, Provenza, Santi ⊘ , Zenato
Foods: Pasta primavera, delicate fish; drinks well on its own.

Müller-Thurgau

This white, from a grape that is a cross between Riesling and Sylvaner, is not for everyone. Young wines are dry to the point of being austere, but in good ones the steeliness softens with a year or so in the bottle, and the wine is attractive with simply prepared fish.

Age: best at 2–3 years
Price: $6.50–10 +
Recommended Producers: Enofriulia, Kettmeir ✳,
Spagnolli Isera ◆
Foods: Trout, sole, herb-flavored goat cheese

Orvieto

This Umbrian white, traditionally made in dry *(secco)* and sweet *(abboccato)* styles, had degenerated into very ordinary stuff until producers like Antinori, Ruffino, and a few others began upgrading quality in the late eighties. Today, Orvieto is one of the best values in Italian whites. Mediocre wines are still made, however, so stick to the producers recommended below. Orvieto is dry, but not severely so like some of the wines of the northeast. The fruit is round and appealing with crisp acidity, and the wines are best when quite young and fresh.

Age: 1 year–18 months
Price: $6.50–8
Recommended Producers: Antinori Campogrande
  ✪, Ruffino ✪, Rocca della Macie, Barbi, Melini,
  Palazzone ◆, Vaselli
Foods: Pastas with cream sauce, fish and seafood,
  rabbit, salads with light vinaigrette

Pinot Bianco

The Pinot Bianco grape is widely grown in northern Italy and results in wines ranging from ordinary to quite stylish and fragrant, depending on the producer. Some of the best come from regions of Friuli and go for considerably more than $12 a bottle; good ones exist for less, but avoid the very cheap ones, which are poor value. In Tuscany the grape may be blended with Chardonnay with excellent results.

Age: 1–2 years
Price: $8–12
Recommended Producers: Enofriulia ◆, La Cadalora ◆, Terlano, Tiefenbrunner, Volpe Pasini,
  Maso Poli, Antinori Bianco Toscana, Ruffino Libaio ✪
Foods: Seafood pastas (but not too spicy), sole and
  similar fish, fettucine Alfredo, chicken with
  cream sauce

Pinot Grigio

One of the most popular whites from Italy but practically unknown in the United States prior to the eighties. Quite dry, with zesty fruit and piquant flavors in the best wines, but mediocre ones—on the increase due to demand—are thin and lack flavor. Produced mainly in the northeast regions of Alto-Adige (where acidity is highest), Trentino, Friuli, and the Veneto. Prices have risen for the better ones, but those over $12 are rarely worth it. Exceptions: Livio Felluga ($15), Abbazia di Rosazzo ($16.50), Jermann. Expect to pay $8.99 to $10.99 for other good ones—snap them up if you find them for less.

Age: 1–2 years, superior vintages
Price: $7–10+
Recommended Producers: Bollini, Bortoluzzi ♦, Boscaini, Casal del Ronco, Collavini, Marina Danieli ♦, Doro Princic, Furlan, Barone Fini, La Cadalora Valagarini ♦, Kettmeir, Lungarotti, Maso Poli, Plozner, San Valentino ✪, Santi, Tiefenbrunner, Torre di Luna
Foods: Seafood, especially shellfish (steamed mussels, clams), pastas with garlic and oil, *pesto* sauce, goat cheese, grilled eggplant

Pomino Bianco

Though made only by Frescobaldi, Pomino has its own DOC appellation in the Chianti Rufina region of Tuscany. This wine, a balanced white blend of Trebbiano, Pinot Bianco, and Chardonnay, used to be better until Frescobaldi siphoned off the best lots for the reserve style "Il Benefizio" ($16), which also contains Chardonnay. It's still a quite decent dry white, however.

Age: 1–3 years
Price: $8–9
Sole Producer: Frescobaldi
Foods: Antipasti, fettucine Alfredo, and light pastas, simple fish and chicken dishes

Sauvignon

Italian Sauvignon Blanc has a crisp, lively fruit that is tart when very young but softens with a year or so in bottle. Most have sharp acidity and grassy aromas that best suit slightly acidic foods; they may, in fact, be too tart for some palates. Top producers in Friuli and the Veneto get well over $12 for their Sauvignons; some are worth it, but many are overpriced.

Other regions, such as Tuscany and Umbria, are starting to experiment with the Sauvignon grape.

Age: 1–2 years, occasionally 3
Price: $8–11
Recommended Producers: Collio, Enofriulia, Furlan, Antinori Borro della Salla ♦, Tiefenbrunner
Foods: Seafood and seafood pastas, goat cheese (including salads and pizzas)

Soave

Can all the wines labeled Soave really be from Soave? Possibly, since the area surrounding the town is choked with vines, but it's questionable. High yields account for the wine's abundance, but it rarely offers more than reasonably clean but neutral flavors, and some are wretched. Bolla is decent and consistent. The best Soave is Soave Classico and Classico Superiore, which cost more but are worth it since they have a bit more character. Only those appellations are recommended here.

Age: 1–2 years, may go 3
Price: $7–10
Recommended Producers: Anselmi, Bisson, Bolla

Castellaro ♦, Boscaini, Masi, Pieropan, Luigi
Righetti, Santa Sofia, Tommasi, Zenato
Foods: Light pastas (seafood, cream sauce, prima-
vera, etc.), fish and seafood, chicken breast

Tocai

In the Veneto and especially Friuli, Tocai is the
favorite white, but it is not well known in the
United States. Its distinctive scent, a mingle of
wildflowers, dried grasses, and hints of almond,
is intriguing, with appealing fruit that is lively
and fresh but surprisingly full-bodied. The good
ones get better with bottle age, and those from
producers like Jermann and Livio Felluga become quite complex. Tocai deserves to be better known here, but it may take a while, as it is
something of an acquired taste.

Age: 1–2 years, may well go 3 or 4
Price: $8–10+
Recommended Producers: Collavini, Marina Dan-
iele ♦, Doro Princic ♦, Marco Felluga, Plozner,
Santa Margherita, Zenato
Foods: Fish and shellfish, Oriental fish and chicken
dishes, spicy pilaf

Torre di Giano

This dry white from the region of Umbria is a
firm, medium-bodied dry wine made from Trebbiano; good value.

Age: 1–2 years
Price: $7–9
Recommended Producer: Lungarotti
Foods: Fish, chicken, pasta

Verdicchio

Another popular white that has grown blander due to excessive demand. Good ones, however, have that brisk, racy fruit that snaps with crispness. Best when quite young and fresh.

Age: 9–18 months
Price: $7.50–10
Recommended Producers: Bucci, Colonnara, Fazi-Battaglia, Garofoli Macrina, Monte Schiavo
Foods: Fish and shellfish

Vernaccia di San Gimignano

Vernaccia has become one of Italy's hottest whites in recent years, and is interesting because it has a rather unusual almond character and can be faintly bitter in aftertaste. Good ones are smooth and round, with lively fruit and flavors that often become more complex with a couple of years in bottle. Part of its charm derives, no doubt, from the picturesque town of San Gimignano that most American tourists visit when they go to Tuscany. Cheaper versions are often bland and lacking in flavor.

Age: 1–3 years
Price: $6–10
Recommended Producers: Giannina, Riccardo Falchini, Guicciardini-Strozzi, Il Cipressino, Pietrafitta, Rigogolo, Monte Oliveto, San Quirico, Teruzzi e Puthod ✪, Angelo del Tufo ✪
Foods: Gnocchi with porcini mushrooms, sole amandine, fish, broiled or poached with light sauce

---

REDS

Good buys abound in Italian reds; there are some real knockouts. Italy makes its share of light, insipid reds (like Bardolino, for instance), but most Italians prefer chewy reds—Barbera, Dolcetto, Rosso di Montalcino, Salice Salentino —reds with big, meaty flavors that are wonderful to drink.

These wines are lesser in stature but not necessarily in weight or concentration. To take an example: Barolo and Barbaresco are the lords of the Piedmont region, but their prices are well above our $10 ceiling. Barbera d'Alba (as well as its fraternal twin, Barbera d'Asti) and Dolcetto are the everyday reds, inexpensive but hearty. Actually, they used to be even less expensive than they are today, but they've been "discovered." Barberas used to go for $5 a bottle, now they're $9 and $10, well above that from some estates. The same is true for Rosso di Montalcino, a red that has zoomed in popularity, and prices are inching upward with each vintage. Some of the increases are due to the exchange rate, though not all. When the dollar bounces back, as it eventually will, prices will stabilize somewhat.

Chianti has gone up too, but so has quality for many Chianti estates. Chianti made its fame as a cheap ($1.50, $1.99 once upon a time) fruity red bottled in straw-covered flasks, and has had a hard time breaking away from that image. Consumers who knew the good wines had the advantage for years because the better wines just couldn't command high prices. The DOC laws themselves hampered upgrading the wines, requiring that the blend for Chianti include the local white varieties, Trebbiano and Malvasia. Once the laws were changed, higher standards favored the better producers, and prices have risen, steeply in some cases.

Happily there are still good Chiantis to be had for $10 or less, even if not as many. And it's a good idea to look out for price cuts on the expensive ones, which happen not infrequently.

Some of the best buys are simple *rossos* (*rosso* is Italian for red), which can be regional wines like Rosso di Montalcino or Rosso Cónero, made by several producers; sometimes they are individual brands, such as Coltibuono Rosso, Rosso della Quercia, or Corvo, and have their own entry as such.

Barco Real

A somewhat lighter but appealing version of Carmignano ($15–20) from Tuscany, and thus similar to Chianti; often beefier; increasingly made, very good value.

Age: 2–3 years
Price: $10+
Sole Producer: Cappezzana ♦
Foods: Roast chicken, grilled meat, lasagna and other meat pastas, pizza

---

Barbera d'Alba
Barbera d'Asti
Barbera del Monferrato

Barbera d'Alba has the largest production and is the richest of the three, a fruity, chewy red that is generally drinkable in its second or third year (tannic ones may need longer). If well balanced, they age nicely six to eight years and are excellent value to buy in quantity. Barbera d'Asti is lighter in density and body, with vivid fruit, also good value. Neither is to be confused with Barbera del Monferrato, which is lighter still and sometimes a bit fizzy *(frizzante)*.

Age: 2–3 years, more concentrated ones age 6–8
Price: $7.50–10
Recommended Producers: Batasiolo, Castello di Neive ♦, Cavallotto, Clerico ♦, Aldo Conterno ♦, G. Cortese, R. Fenocchio ♦, Fontanafredda, Franco Fiorina ♦, Marchesi di Barolo, Mascarello ♦, Prunotto, Renato Ratti, Torregiorgi, Villadoria
Foods: Roast meats and poultry, pizza, meat pastas, sausage and peppers, savory cheeses (Asiago, Bel Paese, Cheddars)

Cabernet

Cabernet Sauvignon is now grown in many parts of Italy and is frequently very expensive, made in styles that stand with the best of California and Bordeaux. The lighter Cabernets of the northeast (Friuli, Trentino, Veneto) were until recently made mostly from Cabernet Franc, but lately are increasingly blended with Cabernet Sauvignon or Merlot—and the better for it. Cabernet Franc alone can be quite light and somewhat thin. There are several DOC zones for Cabernet in Friuli, Trentino, and the Veneto. The lightest wines rarely compete with moderate-priced Cabernets from California, Chile, Bulgaria, but a few can and more will emerge in the next few years.

Age: 2–3 years, occasionally more
Price: $7.50–10
Recommended Producers: Bollini, Casal del Ronco, Cavit Riserva, Durandi, Fantinel, Fiorina Cabernello ♦, Gaierhof, Marco Felluga, K. Martini,

Rojuzza, Santa Margherita, Scarpa, J. Tiefenbrunner, Luigi Valle, Gianni Vescovo
Foods: Roast pork, pasta with wild mushrooms,
meat-sauce pastas

Campo Fiorin ✪

Fine sturdy red from Masi, one of the top producers in the Valpolicella region; full-bodied
and intense, somewhere between the light reds
of Valpolicella and the bigger Amarone. Used to
be a good value but it now is sometimes over
$10 though often discounted.

Age: 3–4 years, will age up to 8
Price: $10+
Producer: Masi
Foods: Broiled beef or lamb, meat stews, game

Centine Rosso

See Rosso di Montalcino

Chianti

When the region of Chianti in Tuscany decided
to upgrade quality, it moved to the highest official category of Italian wines, DOCG (*Denominazione di origine controllata e guarantita*—
name and origin controlled and guaranteed).
Grape yields were lowered under the new rules,
and the wines must now be tasted by a panel
to qualify as Chianti. The result reduced quantities of Chianti by nearly half. Sangiovese
remains the predominant grape for Chianti.
Requirements for using white grapes went
from 10 percent to 2 percent and permit

up to 10 percent of other varieties, including Cabernet Sauvignon, which increases flavor intensity. Quality has jumped, especially for Riservas (better lots of wines that must be aged at least three years before release), but they are also much more expensive. Riservas from small, sought-after estates go for $12 to $16 a bottle, sometimes higher; some Riservas (Monte Vertine, Fontodi, Felsina Berardenga, Ruffino Gold Label, Querceto, Volpaia) can be worth it. Regular Chianti is a moderately light red, still uneven in quality but quite charming from the top producers. Those listed are consistently good; asterisks denote producers whose Riservas are sometimes discounted and therefore excellent value.

Age: 2–4 years; Riservas 4–6, and can go 8 or more
Price: $7–10
Recommended Producers: Antinori ✳, Aziano (Ruffino), Badia a Coltibuono Cetamura, Berardenga-Felsina ✪, Brolio ✳ (Ricasoli), Le Corti, Fontodi, Castello di Gabbiano, Fossi, Frescobaldi (Nippozano), Isole e Olena, Lilliano, Luiano Riserva ✪, Lucignano, Melini, Monte Antico, Il Palazzino, Rocca della Macie ✳, Ruffino, San Felice ✳, San Giusto, San Ripolo, Villa Banfi ✳, Villa Cafaggio ✳, Villa Cerna ✳, Villa Cilnia ✳, di Viticcio ✳
Foods: Pizza, hearty pastas with meat sauce, mushrooms, sausage, liver; Riservas with roast or grilled chicken, steak, game birds, sausage and peppers, veal chops

Coltibuono Rosso ✪

An excellent red from Badia a Coltibuono, one of the top Chianti estates near Siena. Blended from the Chianti red grapes, Sangiovese and

Canaiolo Nero, with a small percentage of Cabernet Sauvignon, this sturdy red is a Super buy.

Age: 3 years, will age 4–6
Price: $8–8.50
Producer: Badia a Coltibuono
Foods: A versatile red, good with pizza, grilled beef, or chicken, other hearty fare

Corvo Rosso

This widely available Sicilian red is consistently agreeable, normally not a qualification sufficient to be included in this book. However, in superior vintages like 1985 and 1988, it proved an exceptional value and is therefore worth considering. (The Bianco is a commercially acceptable white but nothing special.)

Age: 1–3 years
Price: $5–7
Producer: Duca di Salparuta
Foods: Braised chicken or veal, meatballs, lasagne, pizza

Dolcetto d'Alba
Dolcetto di Dogliani

The role of Dolcetto in the Piedmont, whose capital is Milano, is often likened to that of Beaujolais in France. Like Beaujolais, it is a quaffing wine, but much meatier. Dolcetto d'Acqui is lighter and not generally recommended; Dolcettos from Alba and Dogliani are the best. It is unfortunate that Dolcettos from some estates have shot beyond our price limit. Buy these with care. Dolcetto's appeal is its early thrust of flashy, berrylike fruit that balances tannin and acidity. Within two years, however, the cherubic fruit begins to fade, and takes with it the young wine's charm. Catch it before the tannins and acid take over.

Age: 1–2 years, maybe 3 in exceptional vintages
Price: $8–10
Recommended Producers: Elio Altare ♦, Azelia, Batasiolo, Caldi, Casstello di Neive ♦, Cavalotto, Aldo Conterno ✳, Contratto, Flavio Accornero, Fenocchio ♦, Franco Fiorina, Luciano Sandrone ♦, Marchesi di Barolo, Mascarello, Masolino, Fratelli Oddero, Palladino, Paolo Cordero ♦, Quinto Chionetti, La Spinona ♦, Valfieri ♦
Foods: Meat antipasti, cold smoked chicken or turkey, pizza, young savory cheeses like Ricotta Salata, Caprini, Dolcelatte

Freisa

Traditionally this was a light, frizzy, sweetish quaffing red without much appeal outside the Piedmont (though highly popular there). Of late, top producers have shifted to a firmer dry, fruity style that accentuates the strawberry-raspberry flavors. Look for Secco on the label. Promising—*if* it doesn't get too expensive.

Age: 8–18 months
Price: $8–10
Recommended Producers: Aldo Conterno, Franco Fiorina, Fratelli Oddero, Prunotto, Scarpa, Valentino ○, Vietti ♦
Foods: Sausages, *fritto misto* (fried innards and vegetables), cheeses such as Gorgonzola, aged Asiago, Fontina Val d'Aosta

Gattinara

Made from the same grape, Nebbiolo, that produces Barolo, Gattinara is a mild-mannered version of medium body. Quality varies among producers in the region, and sometimes the wines are thin. Good ones, however, are well balanced, flavorful, and can age surprisingly well. Prices have risen considerably in recent years; more expensive ones (♦) are often found on sale.

Age: Drinkable at 3–4 years, can hold to 8, 10, or more
Price: $8–10
Recommended Producers: Antoniolo, Umberto Fiore ♦, L&G Nervi ♦, Travaglini, Vallana ✪
Foods: Roast or grilled meat and poultry, veal scallopini, pasta or risotto with white truffles

Ghemme

A firm red from the Gattinara district of the Piedmont, also made from Nebbiolo and often a better value than either. Production is smaller, however, and it is not widely available.

Age: 4–8 years
Price: $9
Recommended Producers: Le Colline, di Sizzano, Cantalupo, Troglia
Foods: Grilled steak, roast kid, lamb, *ossobuco*

Grumello (see Valtellina)

Inferno (see Valtellina)

Merlot

Merlot is widely grown in Italy, but many of the wines are light and grapey, lacking the plummy fruit character so attractive in good Merlot. Those that do approach a richer style are often priced above $10, but they are occasionally found for less (as noted by the diamond below). Those from Colli Orientali and Colli Goriziano Grave in Friuli are among the best, especially Riservas.

Age: 2–4 years
Price: $8–10
Recommended Producers: Attems ♦, Casal del Ronco, Doro Princic ♦, Fantinel, Marco Felluga, Pietro Rubini, Santa Margherita, Torre di Luna, Luigi Valle, Venica
Foods: rabbit, pork; lamb with Riservas

Monte Antico ✪

Superbuy red from the hills near Montalcino in Tuscany, made from Sangiovese and Canaiolo. Sturdy, rich but well balanced, it ages with some elegance and is superior to some Chianti Riserva.

Age: 3–4 years, will age 6–7
Price: $8–9
Recommended Producers: Castello di Monte Antico, La Pievanella
Foods: Beef, lamb, hearty pastas, game birds

Montefalco Rosso

Firm, appealing red from Umbria, near the town of Montefalco. Best is Rosso d'Arquata, blended from Barbera, Canaiolo, and Merlot, and aged in small oak; attractively robust but little known outside the region. Sagrantino, another red from the same area, is riper, more robust, less refined, and sometimes sweet *(passito)*.

Age: Drinkable at 2–3 years, will age 4–6
Price: $7.50–10
Recommended Producer: Adanti
Foods: Pastas with meat sauce, roast chicken, game birds

Montepulciano d'Abruzzi Rosso

Wines from the Abruzzi region on the Adriatic coast of Italy are coming into their own as consumers discover what good values they are, especially the *rosso,* a deep, vivid red with meaty flavors and just enough tannin to give it "grip." Increasingly, large quantities of this wine mean that some are less impressive; others can be excellent value, such as Rosso della Quercia, and Riservas. Many also come in 1.5-liter magnums, a good all-purpose red for parties.

Age: 1–3 years, the best last 4–6
Price: $5–8
Recommended Producers: Cornaccia, Casal Thaulero ✪, Dario d'Angelo, Illuminati, Monti, Bruno Nicodemi, Rosso della Quercia, Tollo Rubino, Tuscolo, Valenti, Zaccagnini
Foods: Lamb stew, roast chicken, lasagne and other meat pastas, pizza

---

Nebbiolo d'Alba

A sound red from the Nebbiolo grape, occasionally approaching the character of Barolo but softer and lighter in body. Better wines labeled Nebbiolo della Langhe are similar. CAUTION: Both can be thin and hard in lesser vintages; overpriced from some estates, rarely worth more than $10 (exception: Luigi Einaudi, $12), but those that cost more are sometimes found at discount (♦).

Age: 2–4 years, may last 6–8
Price: $9–10
Recommended Producers: Aldo Conterno ♦, Elio Altare ♦, Flavio, Franco Fiorina, Massolino, Oddero, Palladini, Villadoria
Foods: Roast chicken, veal stew, *ossobuco*

Notoparano (see Rosso del Salento)

Refosco

Robust red made from the grape of that name and a favorite hearty quaff in Friuli. Likely to be more widely seen here in the future. Occasionally can be overly tannic; Riservas are better balanced but cost more than $10.

Age: 2–3, can go 5 or 6
Price: $7–9.50
Recommended Producers: Durandi, Fantinel ♦
Foods: Hearty meat stews, game, savory cheeses

Rosso Cónero
Rosso Piceno

Two solid, meaty reds from the Marches region
of central Italy made from Montepulciano and
Sangiovese grapes, these *rossos* can be excellent value. Somewhat tannic when young but
flavorful and well balanced, they often achieve
some elegance with a few years in bottle.

Age: 3 years, will age 6–8
Price: $7–9
Recommended Producers: Cupramontana, Castel-
 fiora ✳, Fazi-Battaglia, Garofoli, Ronchi, Torelli,
 Villamagna ✳, Villa Pigna
Foods: Lamb, beef, game birds, duck

Rosso di Montalcino

Firm, vigorous red wine from the Montalcino
hills, traditionally made from young vines of
Brunello di Montalcino, Tuscany's concentrated, noble (and expensive) red. Now may include lots of Brunello not good enough for the
main label, as well as wines from vines under
ten years old. The increasing popularity of the
rosso has boosted prices beyond our limit for
some of these wines, but it is often an excellent
value from the estates cited.

Age: 2–4 years, can go 6 or 8
Price: $7.50–10
Recommended Producers: Altesino, Avignonesi ♦,
 Banfi Centine, Caprili, Castelgiocondo, Col d'Or-
 cia ⊘, Lisini ♦, Mastroianni, Nardi, La Poderina,
 il Poggiolo ♦, San Filippo, Valdicava
Over $10: Caparzo, Pertimaldi, Talenti, Val di Suga
Foods: Roast or grilled meats, stews, game, savory
 cheeses like aged Asiago, Parmigiano, Scamorze

Rosso del Salento

Strong, sturdy, tannic reds with a faintly bitter edge, from the Salento Peninsula in southern Italy. Often very ripe and high in alcohol (14 percent or better), particularly the best known, Notoparano, which needs six or seven years to become drinkable. Salice Salentino, which has its own DOC, is similar and made from the same grape (Negroamaro), but is a bit leaner and not as brawny. A better buy, in my view.

Age: 6–8 years, can age to 10 or 12
Price: $8–9
Recommended Producers: Notoparano (Cosimo Taurino), Santachiara (Medico), Leone de Castris
Foods: Meat stews, game, particularly venison, pecorino cheese

Rubesco

Solid, meaty red from the Lungarotti estate in Umbria. Made primarily from Sangiovese and drinkable within two to four years of the vintage; Riserva has more depth, but costs more and ages eight to ten.

Age: 2–4 years
Price: $10
Producer: Lungarotti
Foods: Roast meats, game birds, lasagne

Ruffino Il Magnifico

Husky table red from Ruffino, a nonvintage blend that is very inexpensive but consistently sound.

Age: Immediately drinkable
Price: $6
Producer: Ruffino
Foods: Great with pizza, sausage and peppers

Santa Maddalena

Fairly substantial red from the Tyrol region of
Trentino in northern Italy; rich color, meaty flavors with a slight hint of bitterness; solid, occasionally complex; good value.

Age: 3 years, will age to 5 or 6
Price: $8
Recommended Producers: Josef Brigl, Hofstatter,
   Kettmeir, Lageder, San Michele-Appiano
Foods: Meats, game, blood sausage, hearty pastas

Spanna

Earthy, full-bodied red from the Nebbiolo grape
(called Spanna on the lower slopes at Gattinara;
concentrated, even coarse, but ages for years
(undrinkably tannic when under 7 or 8 years).
Generous, expansive fruit, muscular in structure; well-stored old ones can be impressive,
but are less a bargain than formerly; some are
a better value than Gattinara.

Age: 4–5 years, will go to 10 or 15
Price: $6–8
Recommended Producers: Antoniolo, Dessilani,
   Ferrando, Nervi, Travaglini, Vallana
Foods: Meat stews, especially venison, Gorgonzola

Teroldego Rotaliano

Lively dark red from Trentino with ripe, robust fruit; tannic when young but matures within three or four years to become round and smooth. Riservas aged two years.

Age: 2–3 years; Riservas 4–6
Price: $8
Recommended Producers: Gaierhof, Istituto San Michele, Maso Donati, Zeni
Foods: Beef or lamb stew, savory cheese, pasta with meat sauce

---

Valpolicella

Only the *classico superiore* is worth recommending, as ordinary Valpolicella is a modest and often uninteresting light red. Wines from the better producers, however, are nicely balanced, medium-bodied, smooth, fruity reds that can be genial with lighter foods. Beware very cheap ones, which are often thin and lack character. Amarone is this wine's bigger, tougher older brother, made from grapes that are dried to concentrate flavor.

Age: 2 years, can go 3 or 4
Price: $5–7
Recommended Producers: Bertani, Bolla, Boscaini, Guerrieri-Rizzardi, Masi, Luigi Righetti, Santa Sofia, Tedeschi
Foods: Calves' liver, pizza, ragout

Valtellina Superiore

The steep hills of the Valtellina district in Lombardy produce several sturdy reds from Nebbiolo that are similar in structure and flavor: Grumello, Inferno, Sassella, Valgella, which are frequently excellent value. Wines made from extra-ripe grapes and aged longer go under the name Sfurzat, which is very full-bodied and can be somewhat raisiny. Valtellina Rosso, simple but meaty, well balanced, is often a superb value for events like barbecues, or large groups.

Age: 2–3 years, can go 4–6 or longer
Price: $6–9
Recommended Producers: Nino Negri, Nera, Rainoldi, Tona
Foods: Pizza, sausage and peppers, braised beef, *ossobuco*

ITALIAN ROSÉS

Italian *rosato,* as the rosés are called, can be charming. The best ones are dry, crisp, and refreshing; some even have character, such as Rosa del Golfo from Apulia. It's well to realize, however, that some Italian producers now sweeten their *rosatos* to please Americans who like sweet pink wines. Listed below are what I consider the best values in *dry rosatos.* They can accompany a variety of lighter foods, including cold meats, prosciutto, and simple fish. Drink them as young and fresh as possible, in their first or second year.

Castel del Monte Rosato, Apulia, $7
Chiaretto del Garda, Veneto, $7
Coltibuono Rosato, Tuscany, $7.50
Lacryma Rosa, Mastroberardino, Campania, $10 ◆
Lagrein Rosato, dei Conti Martini, Trentino, $6

Rosa del Golfo, Apulia, $10 ◆
Rosa dei Masi, Veneto, $9
Ruffino Rosatello, Tuscany, $7
Silvarosa, Giacosa Donato, Piedmont, $7
Taurino Rosato di Salice Salentino, $8

SUPERBUYS / ITALY

Whites

Anselmi Soave Classico, Veneto, $6.99–$8
Breganze di Breganze, Veneto, $8–10
Coltibuono Bianco, Tuscany, $7.99
Plozner Chardonnay, Friuli, $8.99
Ruffino Libaio, Tuscany, $7.99
J. Tiefenbrunner Chardonnay, Trentino, $7.99
Santi Lugana, Lombardy, $8.50
Antinori Orvieto Campogrande, Umbria, $7
San Valentino Pinot Grigio, $6
Vernaccia di San Gimignano, Tuscany (Angelo
   del Tufo, Teruzzi e Puthod), $5.99–8.99

Reds

Berardenga Felsina Chianti Classico, Tuscany,
   $7.99–8.99
Isole e Olena Chianti Classico, Tuscany, $7.99
Fontodi Chianti Classico, $7.99
Luiano Chianti Classico Riserva, $8
Coltibuono Rosso, Tuscany, $7.50
Valentino Dolcetto d'Alba, Piedmont, $7.99
Monte Antico, Tuscany, $7.99
Col d'Orcia Rosso di Montalcino, Tuscany, $7–9

Spain and Portugal

The best wines of Spain and Portugal are red, and both countries offer some amazing wine values. Portugal's robust, meaty, flavorful reds go for $5 and $6, several Superbuys () among them. Spain's well-known Riojas and Penedés reds still offer a number of bargains among the growing number of more serious, and more expensive, wines.

Neither country does much with white wines, though whites are made in copious quantities. Iberian wine producers have never taken white wines very seriously. Portugal has its Vinho Verde, the young, tart "green wines" of the Minho region bordering the Douro. While they can be delightful and refreshing there, or in Lisbon, or at an oceanside restaurant watching the sunset, many are too light-bodied to travel well over greater distances. Similarly, Spanish whites are agreeable, especially if they are dry and crisp, but they are rarely special. I suspect this will change within a few years. Now that Spain and Portugal are full-fledged members of the European Common Market, we can expect a jump in wine production and, we can hope, better quality across the board.

SPAIN

Some exciting new wines have already begun to appear in Spain. American consumers are familiar with Spanish Rioja and with reds like Torres Sangre de Toro and Coronas. In recent years new vintners and winemakers have emerged from other regions of this vast country —the Ribera del Duero, Navarra, Rueda, La Mancha. But consider: Spain is the third-largest producer of wine in the world, right on the heels of France and Italy. It has more vineyards than either, but we hardly know Spanish wine. Most of it is produced in bulk and consumed within the country itself. La Mancha, for instance, produces over a third of Spanish wine, almost all of it in the 450 cooperatives that dot the region.

Get a taste of rich little reds like Lar de Barros or J. Diaz Madrid, which sell for $6 to $8 a bottle, and you'll get a notion of what Spain can do when a talented winemaker is at the helm. Some of the new wines are expensive. Pesquera, Vina Magaña, and most Ribera del Duero sell for $16 and up, and they are impressive. In Rioja, too, the best ones are pulling away from the pack, but there are still numerous good buys for $10 and under.

CATALONIA

Catalonia produces some of Spain's best wines, especially the reds from the Penedés, including Cabernet Sauvignon from several producers and popular reds from the Torres firm such as Coronas and Sangre de Toro. West of Barcelona, near the town of San Sadurní de Noya, are the largest sparkling-wine producers in the world—Freixenet and Codorníu, as well as other names in Spanish *cavas* such as Juve y Camps, Segura Viudas ✪, Mont Marcal, Lembey ✪, and others.

The leading wines are listed separately.

Cabernet Sauvignon

Rich, earthy, but smooth and drinkable within three to five years for wines that are $10 and under, though they can often hold longer. More expensive Cabernets such as Torres Gran Coronas Black Label need long aging. *Recommended:* Jean Leon, Raimat ✪, Jaume Serra.

Chardonnay

Fairly new to the region. The only one available in our price range is made by Raimat, a dry, oak-aged Chardonnay that can be very agreeable when two to four years old. Jean Leon's very good Chardonnay is more expensive but sometimes marked down, and then an excellent value.

Coronas

A sound, medium-bodied red wine made by the leading Penedés firm, Torres. Gran Coronas is meatier, with more concentrated fruit and flavor. (Gran Coronas Black Label, made from 100 percent Cabernet Sauvignon, is a wonderful wine but out of our league.)

Age: 2–4 years; 5–7 for Gran Coronas
Price: $6–10
Sole Producer: Torres
Foods: Hamburgers, grilled chicken

Sangre de Toro ✪

Another great value from Torres, Sangre de Toro is a robust, fruity red, immediately drinkable. The Reserva is even more so, full of berryish fruit and vigorous body that is excellent with hearty dishes like meat stews or barbecued meats.

Age: 2–3 years, up to 5 or more for the Reserva
Price: $5–8
Foods: Hamburgers, grilled meats, chicken, sausages

Viña Sol

A dry, fruity white from Torres, simple but fresh and well made. Somewhat better, due to the addition of Chardonnay, is the Gran Viña Sol ✪, a terrific value and one of the best Spanish whites.

Age: 1–3 years
Price: $4–7
Sole Producer: Torres
Foods: Mild fish and seafood

Lar de Barros

This chewy, drinkable red from Extremadura in western Spain is an excellent value from the province's only official appellation, Tierra de Barros. Rich, sturdy fruit makes it a Superbuy.

Age: 4–6 years, will go 10
Price: $7.99
Producer: Bodegas Enviosa Lar de Barros ✪
Foods: Roast or grilled meats, meat stews, savory
  cheeses such as Manchego

La Mancha

Huge quantities of nondescript wines are produced in La Mancha, much of it in bulk that supplies everyday wines all over Spain. The plains of La Mancha have more than a million acres in vines, constituting Spain's largest appellation. Best known in the United States are jugs of Valdepeñas, light reds that are usually served chilled in Spain to make them more refreshing and quaffable. A few producers make sturdier reds of firmer structure aged in oak (Felix Solis) that may soon find their way here.

Navarra

Navarra, north of the Rioja and west of Catalonia, produces reds similar to Rioja from some of the same grapes, Garnacha (Grenache) and Tempranillo. Supple, generously fruity new reds have emerged here recently, offering good everyday drinking value. Be on the watch also for Navarra's dry, bracing rosés (labeled *rosado*), great favorites of Hemingway on his frequent trips to Pamplona.

Age: 2–4 years
Price: $5–7.50
Recommended Producers: Las Campanas Navarra
   Crianza, Julián Chiuite, Ochoa Navarra Crianza,
   Señorio de Sarria Reserva and Gran Reserva ✪
Foods: Grilled meats, hamburgers, cheese

Ribera del Duero

This region, west of the Rioja and near Valla-
dolid in Old Castile, produces Spain's most intense and expensive red, Vega Secilia, which
sells for $50 to $60 a bottle. Other producers
have sprung up, a few producing hearty reds
more in our price range, but often quite meaty
and long-lived. Watch for them on sale or at
discount stores.

Age: 4–10 years, or longer
Price: $8–10+ ✳
Recommended Producers: Balbas ✪, Bodegas
   Mauro ♦, Penalba ✪, Señorio de Nava, Viña
   Pedrosa ♦
Foods: Steak, grilled meats, meat stews

Rioja

Spain's best-known wine region, producing red
wines of the same name. There are dozens of
producers, about forty of which export to the
United States. Variations in quality abound.
Some of the top estates can command higher
prices, putting their Reservas and Gran Reservas fairly well out of reach. Young Rioja (released after two years, it is called Crianza) is
medium-bodied, fruity, and rather light. Reservas, aged four to six years, are riper and bigger,

as are Gran Reservas, which are the best lots of a superior vintage. Competition has heated up in the last few years, and quality seems to be improving among the leading producers, with good values at the simple level, even better ones among Reservas, which are frequently found marked down.

Age: 3–5 years for Crianza, 5–10 for Reservas, Gran Reservas, and some beyond that
Price: $6–10+
Recommended Producers: Berberana, Bilbainas, Bosconia, Campo Viejo, CUNE, Gran Condal, La Rioja Alta, Lopez de Heredia, Loriñon, Marqués de Arienzo ❂, Marqués de Caseres, Marqués de Riscal, Martinez- Bujanda, Montecillo, Olarra, Bodegas Palacio Glorioso ❂, Paternina, Valdemar, Vina Tondonia
Foods: Lamb, beef, savory cheeses like Manchego

Rioja Blanco and Rosado

Most whites and rosés from Rioja lag well behind the red wines in quality, though a few (Bilbainas, Cumbrero, Cune, Martinez-Bujanda) show a certain dash and freshness in recent vintages. Look for the youngest, a year or two at most.

Rueda

Another region in Old Castile, up and coming for crisp, dry, flavorful white wines made from the Verdejo grape. Much more stylish and appealing than Rioja Blanco—perhaps the reason several Rioja producers are now making their whites there.

Age: 1–3 years
Price: $7–10
Recommended Producers: Marqués de Griñon ◆,
   Marqués de Riscal, Martinsancho ✪, Martivilli,
   Vega de la Reina
Foods: Fish, seafood

Toro ✪

This new region in Old Castile is creating a lot
of excitement with its bargain-priced hearty
reds like Gran Colegiata, an amazing buy at $5!
Toro is hot, so prices will undoubtedly rise, but
perhaps not too high too fast. Snap them up!
And watch for new labels that may appear.

Age: 3–10 years
Price: $5–6
Recommended Producers: Fariña Gran Colegiata
   ✪, Luis Mateos Vega de Toro ✪
Foods: Hearty meat dishes

OTHER GOOD BUYS

Spain has a number of other excellent values
from various parts of this large country. The
ones below are highly recommended and include a few Superbuys.

J. Diaz Colmenar Madrid ✪, $6, a dark, chewy
   red with heaps of flavor.
Palacio de Leon Tinto, $5, firm, deep, and
   tannic, with good aging potential.
Montesierra Somontano, $7, Spain's answer to
   Beaujolais, light, fruity, and appealing.
Estola La Mancha Reserva, $6–8, berryish

fruit, with toasty oak overtones; very
drinkable.

Marqués de Caro Tinto, $6.50, lively, appealing
red.

Raimat Merlot, $10, a nicely balanced medium-
weight red from the Penedés of Catalonia.

René Barbier Red Table Wine ✪, $3.50, top
bargain for everyday red.

Taja Jumilla Tinto ✪, $5, robust, lively and
fruity.

PORTUGAL

As in Spain, it is the red wines of Portugal that
generate the most interest—astonishment, actually. What a shock to find rich, meaty, pow-
erfully structured reds with such incredibly
cheap price tags! At full markup they rarely go
beyond $7.99 a bottle; usually, however, they
are priced well below that at $4, $5, and $6.
Certainly they are among the most undervalued
of wines—or is it just that we have gotten used
to *over*priced wines? While the latter is unde-
niably true, there are other factors at work. One
has to do with image. Portuguese reds lack the
slick image of wines from Italy, France, or California that may be comparable in style but can
command higher prices. People see the low
prices for wines like Dão, Serradayres, Periquita, and various Garrafeiras, and wonder how
they can be any good.

Those who have discovered the good ones,
however, feel they have been let in on a great
secret and are delighted by the bold, robust flavors. That brings up another factor. Most Portuguese reds are rustic and full-bodied, dark,
and often rather tannic, and thus not to every-

one's taste. If you like that style, however, you will find some extraordinary buys. Portuguese reds can be very long-lived. You will see many wines that are ten to fifteen years old, but most are drinkable when they arrive here, and often quite glorious. Some, however, have spent too long in wood, and you may find they have lost fruit or dried up. The recent trend is to emphasize fruit rather than wood, producing wines that are ready to drink within a few years, but can age a decade or more. Keep an eye on Portugal. It is a wine industry that is starting to churn with new energy, and some Portuguese vintners are beginning to produce reds with more finesse. Prices for some of them are already on the rise.

In Portugal wines go by regional appellation, such as Dão or Bairrada, but many are better known by producer or by proprietary names. This is especially true for reds from the regions of Ribatejo and Alentejo, for example. The wines recommended are listed alphabetically by region, type, producer, or brand name, depending upon which identity is strongest and most easily recognized.

Alentejo. This large region southeast of Lisbon near the Spanish border is best known for medium- to full-bodied red wines, and whites of lesser interest. Large cooperatives such as Borba, Reguengos de Moussaraz, and Redondo make solid, meaty reds that are very good value, but serious estates have begun to appear in recent years. The future promises some exciting wines.

Age: 5–8 years
Price: $5–8

Recommended Producers: Borba, Borba Reserva
   ✪ , Herdade de Esporão Tinto, Herdade de Santa
   Marta Tinto, João Pires Anfora ✪ , Redondo Real
   Lavrador, Reguengos de Monsaraz, Reguengos
   Reserva ✪
Foods: Hearty meat dishes, game, stews, savory
   cheeses

Anfora ✪. Rich, full-bodied red from the Pal-
mela district of Alentejo. Ripe flavors, soft tannins, a Superbuy from João Pires.

Age: 3–5 years, will go to 8 or 10
Price: $7
Sole Producer: João Pires
Foods: Grilled meats, stews, savory cheeses

Bairrada. A region along Portugal's central
coast north of Lisbon noted for well-balanced
red wines, especially Reservas. These reds are
some of Portugal's most elegant, sometimes
compared to Bordeaux in terms of structure
and style. There are excellent values here,
but prices for some wines are inching beyond
$10.

Age: 5–10 years, longer for Reservas
Price: $8–10+
Recommended Producers: Caves Aliança Garra-
   feira ✪ , Caves Primavera, Caves São João ✪ ,
   Caves Velhas, Dom Teodosio Reserva ✪ , Frei
   João Reserva ✪ , Luis Pato, Porta Ferrea, So-
   grape Terra Franca ✪ (also Terra Franca Garra-
   feira), Sousellas Reserva ✪
Foods: Grilled or roast lamb or beef, prime rib

Bucelas. A small region near Lisbon that produces dry white wines of medium body. Few
reach the United States, though recent plantings

in the region may change that. For now, none
recommended.

Casal de Azenha ✪**.** B. Paulo da Silva's brand
name for a ripe, meaty red from vineyards near
the region of Colares (see below). Deep and
long-lived (ten to fifteen years).

Age: **10–15 years**
Price: **$7–10**
Sole Producer: **B. Paulo da Silva**
Foods: **Game, meat stews**

Catariña ✪**.** A very attractive dry white wine
from João Pires; fruity, crisp, and flavorful, with
a hint of Chardonnay in the blend.

Age: **1–2 years**
Price: **$6**
Producer: **João Pires**
Foods: **Fish, seafood**

Colares. This small region on the Atlantic coast
above Lisbon was once noted for dark, rich reds
that needed many years of aging. Recent wines
are lighter, fruitier, and more supple; agreeably
good, but rarely more—exception: Casal de
Azenha, a Superbuy from vineyards just inland
from Colares.

Age: **5–10 years**
Price: **$5–8**
Recommended Producers: **B. Paulo da Silva** ✪**, Ta-
    vares y Rodrigues**
Foods: **Beef, lamb, meat stews**

Conde de Santar ✪**.** An estate-bottled Dão,
and one of the best, with chewy fruit and good
depth of flavor.

Age: 4–8 years
Price: $9
Producer: Conde de Santar
Foods: Grilled meats, stews, game

Cova da Ursa ✪. A wood-aged Chardonnay from the firm of João Pires; one of Portugal's best dry whites, evidence of the country's potential for superior white wine.

Age: 2–4 years
Price: $8
Producer: João Pires
Foods: Fish, shellfish, veal or chicken in cream sauce

Dão. One of Portugal's oldest and best-known regions for sturdy, full-bodied red wines, and to a lesser extent, dry whites. In northern Portugal, just south of the Douro region, it is a region somewhat in transition. Traditionally the hearty red Dão were given lengthy aging in cask, resulting in heavy, tannic wines that tasted more of wood than fruit. Quality still varies among the numerous large producers who buy grapes and bottle the wines under brand names. There are, however, some excellent Reservas and Garrafeiras. For a long time the only estate was Conde de Santar (a Superbuy), but now other producers have purchased vineyards that will appear under estate names. Be wary of wines over eight to ten years old. Dão can certainly age at least that, but some wines may be dried out.

Age: 5–8 years, longer for Reservas, Garrafeiras
Price: $4–8
Recommended Producers: Caves Aliança, Borges & Irmão Meia Encosta, Caves Velhas Garrafeira ✪,

Conde de Santar ✪, Dom Teodosio Cardeal Reserva, Fonseca Terras Altas ✪, Grão Vasco Reserva, Herdeiros General Santos Costa (Caves Imperiore), Porta Dos Cavaleiros Garrafeira

Foods: Feijoada (Brazilian meat stew) and other robust meat dishes, savory cheeses

Douro. The steep slopes of the Douro Valley in northern Portugal are most famous for Port, the fabulous fortified red. But a few producers also make red table wine that is big, deep, and dark, as one might expect from this rugged region. Very concentrated Douro reds, such as Barca Velha, are now quite expensive, but a couple can be found within our price range.

Age: Drinkable 5–8 years but often need much longer

Price: $9–10+

Recommended Producers: Caves Accacio Reserva, Ferreirinha Esteva ✪, and Reserva Especial, Quinta do Cotto

Garrafeira, Reserva, Particular. Many producers make a Garrafeira, or proprietor's reserve, which is the producer's best. The wine may be made from the best lots of a regional wine such as Bairrada or Dão, or it may be a nonspecific blend of exceptional wines. Some are labeled Garrafeira Particular, others Reserva Particular. Wines from top producers such as those listed below are deep, rich, well balanced, and long-lived. They are some of the best Portugal has to offer, yet rarely exceed $10 a bottle.

Age: 7–10 years, can go 12

Price: $7.50–10

Recommended Producers: Antonio Bernardino,

Caves Aliança, Carvalho Ribeiro & Ferreira ✪,
Casaleiro, B. Paula da Silva, Caves São João ✪,
Caves Solar das Francesas, Caves Dom Teodosio,
Caves Velhas ✪
Foods: Roast meats, venison, boar, pheasant, wild
duck

João Pires ✪. Brand name for Caves João Pires
White Muscat, a dry, delightfully fruity white
that is Portugal's top buy in white wine. Fresh,
crisp, and fragrant, with the enticing floral/spice
aromas and flavors of Muscat at its best. What
sets this wine apart from all other Portuguese
whites is that it is utterly clean and beautifully
balanced. Drink it young, within a year of the
vintage if possible, when the fruit is freshest.

Age: 6–18 months
Price: $6.50
Producer: João Pires
Foods: Great by itself

Periquita ✪. An excellent meaty red produced
by José Maria da Fonseca from the Periquita
grape. Fonseca made the Periquita famous with
this wine, one of Portugal's best-known reds
and a Superbuy at under $7.

Age: 5–10 years or longer
Price: $7–10
Producer: José Maria da Fonseca
Foods: Lamb, beef, meat stews

Quinta de Abrigada. A robust red from Portugal's eastern frontier region of Extremadura.
Very good, especially the Garrafeira.

Age: 5–8 years, longer for the Garrafeira
Price: $7–10

Producer: Quinta de Abrigada
Foods: Grilled meats, game

Quinta da Bacalhõa Cabernet Sauvignon.
This fifteenth-century estate just south of Lisbon in Azeitão is owned by the Scoville family, Americans who bought and restored the estate in the 1930s. Cabernet Sauvignon and Merlot were planted in 1975 by the Scovilles' grandson, Thomas. Mostly Cabernet with about 20 percent Merlot, Quinta da Bacalhõa is aged in small oak. Well balanced and flavorful, it found immediate acceptance in the United States due to its appealing drinkability. The price has risen, but it is still an excellent buy.

Age: 4–6 years
Price: $8.75 ✳
Producer: Quinta da Bacalhõa
Foods: Lamb, duck, game birds

Quinta da Camarate Clarete. A light, fruity red from the J. M. Fonseca firm at Azeitão, made in part with Cabernet Sauvignon. Good value.

Age: 2–4 years
Price: $5
Producer: J. M. Fonseca
Foods: Roast chicken, sausages

Quinta da Folgorosa. A very fine estate red from the north central hills of the Torres Vedras region. Folgorosa, owned by the excellent firm of Carvalho, Ribeiro & Ferreira, produces a rich ruby red, full of spicy, cherrylike fruit braced with firm tannins that make it seem more robust than it actually is.

Age: 4–8 years
Price: $7
Producer: Quinta da Folgorosa
Foods: Roast beef, game birds, goat cheese

Ribatejo. A region northeast of Lisbon in the province of Extremadura bordering Spain. Several superb values in red wines are made here, better known by brand names than by the regional name, such as Romeira and Serradayres. Sturdy, rich, often rather Rhônelike in their ripe, oaky flavors and powerful structure.

Age: 4–7 years, Garrafeiras will go 10 or more
Price: $5–8
Recommended Producers: Carvalho, Ribeiro & Ferreira Serradayres Tinto ✪ (the white is also agreeable), C. R. & F. Garrafeira, Caves Velhas Romeira and Romeira Garrafeira ✪, Quinta do Alorna, Dom Teodosio Casaleiro Velho
Foods: Roast meats, game, meat stews

Serradayres ✪. One of the top values in Portuguese reds, this full-bodied, richly textured wine is from a vineyard overlooking the Tagus River in the Ribatejo (see) region bordering Spain. Produced by Carvalho, Ribeiro & Ferreira, Serradayres is the name of the vineyard and means "mountain of air." Well balanced, flavorful, and highly drinkable, it goes for the rather amazing price of $5 a bottle!

Vinho Verde. These very light-bodied, crisp whites (*vinho verde* literally means "green wines") from the northern region of the Minho River can be delightful in Portugal, tart and briskly dry, fresh and bracing. Unfortunately, few taste as good when they arrive here in the United States. They are frequently either over-

sulphured or sweetened to make them seem
less austere. Both practices defeat the purpose;
prices have gone up as well, unjustifiably in my
view, so I recommend very few of these wines.

Age: 12–18 months
Price: $5–8.50
Recommended Producers: Aveleda Grinalda, Casa-
leiro, Casal Garcia, Paco de Teixeiro

FORTIFIED WINES

In Sherry, Port, and Madeira, Spain and Portugal produce the world's greatest fortified wines,
altogether unique in character. They are imi-
tated in wine regions the world over, but most
of the imitators fall well short of the prototypes.
There are not many that can be recommended
here because prices have risen in recent years.
But there are certain ones that fall within our
$10 limit, and I strongly urge you to try them.
You'll probably want to keep a bottle or two on
hand.

Many Sherries cost under $10 a bottle,
though the best have risen beyond that; here, I
only recommend those that I consider truly superior buys.

As for Port, few indeed can be found for $10
—that I would recommend, at any rate. Most of
the Port shippers produce inexpensive wood-
aged Ports labeled Ruby, Tawny, or White Port.
But it's better to spend a dollar or two more and
get a Reserve-style wood Port, as recommended
below (♦). Real Tawny Ports are costly, usually
considerably more than $10—don't be fooled
by Tawnies that are actually a blend of Ruby
and White Port.

Madeira, long undervalued, is also rising in price as consumers discover how delectable it can be. The rich, golden sweet Malmseys have jumped to $20 and $30 a bottle, especially those ten years or older. The lighter Rainwaters, Verdelhos, and Sercials often go for $11 to $12 but occasionally can be found for less.

Sherry
Emilio Lustau Fino (dry) ✪
Emilio Lustau Palo Cortado (off-dry) ✪
Emilio Lustau Pedro Ximenez (very sweet)
Emilio Lustau Amontillado Escuadrilla (off-dry) ✪
Emilio Lustau Cream Sherry (sweet)
Gonzales Byass Tio Pepe Fino (dry)
Pedro Domecq La Ina Fino (dry)
Pedro Domecq Celebration Cream (sweet)
Sandeman Character Oloroso (off-dry, rich)
Sandeman Armada Cream
Vinicola Hidalgo La Gitana Manzanilla (dry)

Port (wood-aged)
Cockburn Special Reserve ✳
Fonseca Bin 27 ✳
Sandeman Founder's Reserve ✳
Warre's Warrior ✳

Madeira (Rainwater, Verdelho, Sercial, Bual, Malmsey)
Blandy (Duke series)
Cossart Gordon
Leacock

SUPERBUYS / SPAIN AND PORTUGAL

Spanish White
Torres Gran Viña Sol, Spain, $8
Marqués de Riscal Rueda, $7.50
Martinsancho Rueda, $7.99

Spanish Red
Torres Sangre de Toro, $5

J. Diaz Colmenar, $5.50
Balbas Ribera del Duero, $8–9
Rioja (Añares, Berberana, Bodegas Palacio),
    $6–8
René Barbier Red Table Wine, $3.50
Toro Fariña Gran Colegiata, $5
Taja Jumilla Tinto, $5
Montesierra Somontano, $5.50
Emilio Lustau Sherry (Fino, Palo Cortado,
    Amontillado)

Portugal White
João Pires White Muscat, $6
João Pires Catariña, $6
Cova da Ursa Chardonnay, $7.99

Portugal Red
Borba Reserva, $7
João Pires Anfora, $6.99
Bairrada (Caves São João, Frei João Reserva,
    Terra Franca, Dom Teodosio Reserva), $7–8
Casal de Azenha, $8
Colares Paulo da Silva, $7
Conde de Santar Dão, $9
Cave Velhas Dão Garrafeira, $7.99
Fonseca Terras Altas, $8
Ferreirinha Esteva Douro, $9
Garrafeira (Carvalho Ribeiro & Ferreira, Caves
    São João, Caves Velhas), $7.50–9.99
Fonseca Perequita, $6–7
Quinta da Bacalhôa Cabernet Sauvignon, $7–
    8.50
Romeira Garrafeira, $7.49
Serradayres Tinto, $6–7

5

Eastern Europe and the Mediterranean

Many wine drinkers have wondered if *perestroika* will result in a more copious flow of wine from Eastern Europe. Undoubtedly it will, though it may take a year or so more for new developments to make an appearance here. For years, varietals from Romania and Bulgaria have offered good value, especially for Cabernet Sauvignon, Merlot, and Chardonnay of Bulgaria. These wines sell for $3 to $5 a bottle—rock-bottom prices, but it wouldn't matter a hoot if the wines were less than decent. The Romanian Premiat wines are at least that; the Bulgarian varietals are often considerably better. A few from other Eastern bloc countries, such as Cabernet Franc from Hungary, Cabernet and Merlot from Yugoslavia, are also surprisingly good, and have the potential to be even better.

Here in the West we have a lot to learn about

Eastern European wines. These countries have, in fact, a long tradition of winegrowing that goes back several centuries. Though most of the wine is produced at large, state-owned wineries. favorable microclimates and highly regarded vineyards do exist. New plantings of popular varietals (Chardonnay, Merlot, Pinot Noir, the Cabernets) as well as classic techniques of vinification and aging in small oak barrels are already under way. In the future we can expect to see more oak-aged wines and Reserve wines that are higher in quality.

The Mediterranean

Greece (including Cyprus), Israel, Algeria, even Lebanon, export wine to the United States. Morocco also produces wine, but it is not available here, though there are agreeable light reds and rather better dry rosés that are quite pleasant to drink there.

Greece, where according to legend the gods first gave wine to man, has been making it so long that the Greeks seem rather laid-back about the whole thing. Most Greek wine is at least palatable (except perhaps for the acquired taste of Retsina, the resinated Greek specialty), but lately a few enterprising producers have begun to revive ancient distinctive grape varieties (such as Xinomavro Naoussis) and, in some cases, use popular grapes like Cabernet, Merlot, and Syrah to blend with them. The results are stylish new wines that offer more flavor and character than simple reds and whites like Demestica, the most widely distributed Greek wines.

Because of limited availability of wines from Eastern Europe and the Mediterranean wine-

producing countries, they are covered briefly
below, beginning with the countries of Eastern
Europe.

Austria. Austria is making a slow comeback in
the United States after several years of re-
trenching. Not many Austrian wines are available here now, but the quality is good. Look for
fresh, light German-style whites with names
like Gumpoldskirchener, Grüner Veltliner, and
Rieslings from leading wine towns like Krems,
Oggauer, and Rust. Austria produces lovely
late-harvest, Botrytised Rieslings; many labeled
Auslese are underpriced and excellent value.
Austria is also experimenting with some success
in red wines made from Cabernet Sauvignon,
Merlot, and Pinot Noir.

Siegendorf and Fritz Salomon are among the
top producers.

Bulgaria. Trakia's meaty Cabernet Sauvignon
(✪) and dry, full-bodied Chardonnay (✪) are
two Superbuys, as lots of American wine lovers
have already discovered. New efforts with Reserve-style wines and barrel-fermented, oak-
aged whites are under way in Bulgaria, which
promise to bring us even more interesting and
complex wines, such as the Chardonnay and
Cabernet Sauvignon labeled Balkan Crest, quite
good values at around $6. Trakia Riesling and
Merlot Blush are simple and adequate. Best
buys ($4.29–5) are:

Trakia Cabernet Sauvignon ✪: meaty, flavorful, well balanced

Trakia Chardonnay ✪: dry, lively, fruity, good
balance and Chardonnay character

Hungary. Don't judge Hungarian wines by the popular red labeled Egri Bikavér (Bull's Blood), now a pallid version of the staunch red it used to be. It ranges from average to good, but is not consistent. Newer, more vigorous and flavorful reds are being made from Cabernet Franc, Merlot, and Cabernet Sauvignon. These wines are not widely available yet, but are good value. Dry Tokay Számarodni can be pleasantly fruity and crisp (best within two years of the vintage), but the most famous Tokay is sweet and the best is expensive. Avoid the cheap ones, which are quite mediocre.

Recommended: Cabernet Franc, Merlot Old
  Vines ✪, Cabernet Sauvignon in reds; Gewürz-
  traminer and Tokay Szármorodni in whites
Price: $5–5.50

Romania. Romania makes far more wine than you would guess based on what is available here. Varietals shipped under the Premiat brand include attractive but mild Cabernet Sauvignon and Merlot, and fair-to-average Sauvignon Blanc and Chardonnay. The Tarnave Riesling, however, is mediocre, and the Pinot Noir quite light. It remains to be seen if Romania can come up with wines as impressive as those of Bulgaria.

Recommended: Premiat Cabernet Sauvignon,
  Merlot
Price: $3–4

Yugoslavia. Yugoslavia has loads of potential for producing exceptional wine. Traditional reds from native grapes like Babíc, Plavac, and Prokupac are robust and meaty, unusual, and often distinctive. Considerable promise, however, lies with such varieties as Cabernet, Merlot, Sauvignon Blanc, and Chardonnay. Good, lively reds made from Merlot and Cabernet Sauvignon are being made in Istria, Slovenia, and the southern area of Kosovo. We aren't seeing much in the United States as yet, but are sure to in the near future.

Recommended: **Canterbury Merlot** ✪
Price: **$8**

GREECE

Things are looking up for Greek wine. Producers of stylish reds and whites like Boutari are likely to prompt a general upgrading of quality as these wines gain wider acceptance. The wines of Greece and the island of Cyprus are known mostly by producer, labeled with descriptive (Dry Red), regional (Naoussa), or proprietary names (Lac des Roches). There are also a few generics such as Retsina, Roditys, Mavrodaphne, or Commanderia. Listings are by the name most appropriate.

Boutari. Producer of several wines of top quality, both white and red, made in styles for immediate drinking. Some of the reds, such as Boutari Grande Reserve or Naoussa, are capable of aging a few years in bottle. Boutari has been dedicated to reviving some of the ancient Greek grape varieties, such as the sturdy red Xinomavro from Náousa or the Negoska, produced in regions of Macedonia. The firm also produces attractive dry white wines, the best among them being Lac des Roches.

Age: Immediately drinkable
Price: $5–7.50
Recommended Wines: Red: Cava, Goumenissa, Paros, Grande Reserve, Naoussa, Patmos. White: Lac des Roches
Foods: Lamb, grilled meats with the reds; with the white, fish, seafood, chicken, roast or grilled vegetables

---

Carras. Porto Carras is another producer of interesting new wines that bear watching, particularly the vigorous, somewhat Bordeauxlike Chateau Carras red and the Carras Reserve dry white. Chateau Carras, made from Cabernet Sauvignon, is quite tannic in some vintages, and age-worthy. This large estate also produces several soft, drinkable, and attractive wines under the Côtes de Meliton label.

Age: Immediately drinkable, though Chateau Carras will age a decade
Price: $4–6
Recommended Wines: Chateau Carras, Domaine Carras Vin Rouge, Carras Reserve Dry White, Carras Rosé Special
Foods: Reds: Grilled meats, hamburgers, pizza; white, rosé: shellfish, cold chicken, picnic foods

---

Commanderia. The sweet amber dessert wine of Cyprus dates back several hundred years to the days of Richard the Lionhearted, who once visited the island. All of the top firms make the wine, which gets its distinctive character from grapes laid out on mats to dry and concentrate in the sun. Though not fortified, it is fairly alcoholic, up to 15 percent. Smooth and not overly sweet, the best ones make a delicious dessert wine.

Age: **Immediately drinkable but can keep several**
   months
Price: **$10+**
Recommended Producers: **Etko, Keo, Loel, Sodap**
Foods: **Desserts, dried fruit, light cake or cookies;**
   alone

Mavrodaphne. The sweet red wine made from
the Mavrodaphne grape. Rich and full-bodied,
it can be delightful when well made, but very
cheap ones can be disappointing.

Age: **Immediately drinkable**
Price: **$5–7**
Recommended Producers: **Achaia Clauss, Boutari,**
   Bouzouki
Foods: **Savory cheese or by itself**

Retsina. The Greek specialty, resin-flavored
and pretty much an acquired taste. Boutari
makes the best one, which is dry, well balanced,
and fruity without an excess of the resin taste.

Age: **1–2 years**
Price: **$3–3.25**
Recommended Producers: **Boutari ✪, Cambas**

Rosé. Greece makes brisk dry rosé; the best
currently is Roditys, which has firm, rather austere fruit with a slight bite. It is quite refreshing,
however, and is versatile with a variety of
Greek foods. Amazingly cheap.

Age: **1–2 years, the younger the better**
Price: **$2–4**
Recommended Producers: **Cambas Roditys, Bou-**
   tari, Rotonda Rosé, Carras Rosé Special
Foods: **Greek appetizers, stewed lamb, feta cheese**

Samos. A sweet white Muscat made on the island of Samos, and quite a delicious way to end a Greek meal or savor a summer afternoon. It is usually served barely cool, yet isn't cloying.

Age: Immediately drinkable
Price: $5–7
Producer: Cooperatives Vinicoles de Samos
Foods: Light cake or cookies; preferably by itself or with fresh fruit

6

United States

California produces 90 percent of the wines made in America. Since California wines are also the most widely distributed of American wines, they are listed first. Following California is a section on good values from other states.

Except for the growing category of premium blends with proprietary names (expensive wines like Opus One, Rubicon, Carmenet, Le Cigare de Volant), California's best wines are labeled with varietal names, as alphabetized below—Cabernet Sauvignon, Chardonnay, Chenin Blanc, etc. There are no jugs, as such, included here, though some of the wines recommended come in 1.5-milliliter magnums. This is not a reflection of some kind of snobbism. Jug wines, especially generics labeled Chablis, Burgundy, Vin Rosé, and the like, once offered good value in American wines. Fairly decent grapes sometimes went into them.

Today, however, jugs have declined both in quality and popularity for various reasons. One is that people want more flavor and character in the wine they drink, even on an everyday basis. The generic jugs are bland, lacking in character, and often lacking in freshness and liveliness. Further, they are rarely vintage-dated, so that you have no idea how old they actually are. Many are pasteurized to keep them stable and give them long shelf life. This treatment robs them of any character or style they might possess and makes them quite dull. Though they are cheap, there is rarely anything beyond that to recommend them. Some producers are aware of this perception of their product; perhaps we shall see some renewed efforts at improvement, but I am not hopeful.

In their place we have a few premium generic blends made from the better grape varieties like Cabernet, Chardonnay, Sauvignon Blanc, Gewurztraminer, and others, such as Trefethen Eshcol White, Preston Estate Red, and The Monterey Vineyard Classics. The best of these wines are included in Proprietary Reds and Proprietary Whites. The big change in California wine over the last two decades has been the shift to varietal wines. Today there are a multitude of moderate-priced varietals, some as bland and characterless as any of the jugs, to be sure, but others that offer good to outstanding value at prices ranging from $4 to $10. This category has ballooned phenomenally in recent years, with a new term coined to target it.

The "Fighting Varietals"

Certain varietal wines have always been under $10. Wines like Sauvignon Blanc, Pinot Blanc,

Zinfandel, Petite Sirah, Chenin Blanc, Johannisberg or White Riesling have usually cost less
than Cabernet Sauvignon, Chardonnay, Merlot, and Pinot Noir, and well under $10. In the
early 1980s, due to a surplus of good-quality
Cabernet and Chardonnay, a new category of
moderate-priced Cabernets and Chardonnays
emerged. Some were second labels of well-
known premium wineries, such as the Liberty
School label of Caymus. But the grape surplus
at that time also spawned a new type of producer, the American version of the French *négociant* (shipper), who bought grapes (or wine)
from various regions, bottled it, and sold it
under such labels as Stratford, Domaine St.
George, J. Wile.

Priced at $5 to $7, these wines were dubbed
the "fighting varietals"—a sobriquet that took
note of their fiercely competitive pricing. Restaurants began pouring them by the glass, especially Chardonnay. People soon learned that
Chardonnay offered more flavor than the average "house" white. Gradually consumers looking to move beyond the jugs discovered these
less expensive varietals, and the category has
taken off. Some of the *négociant* labels now
include Merlot, Sauvignon Blanc, and Pinot
Noir.

Quality varies within this large group of
wines. Not all of them are good, by any means,
but recommended here are those I have found
to be consistently so—so far. I am, however,
disappointed in two developments related to
the fighting varietals. First, some have not main-
tained their quality as production has increased. Liberty School, for instance, a second
label of Caymus, was long one of the best of this
genre, producing Cabernet Sauvignon and

Chardonnay that were superb values. Caught up in the dramatic surge of demand, production doubled, then doubled again; and in the scramble for grapes, quality has suffered. Recently Liberty School cut back production to manageable levels and has regained its former quality —but the price has increased to $10.

Second, several of the best-sellers—Domaine St. George, Christophe, and Round Hill—have started making "Reserve" wines that sell for $10 or more. For the most part these wines are rip-offs—harsher, more tannic Cabernets, oakier, more alcoholic Chardonnays, and nowhere near as drinkable as the regular wines. Worse, some of the regular wines from these producers are now being compromised because the so-called Reserves are skimming off the best grapes. This is commercialism at its worst.

With the rather large surplus of wine that exists at the moment, there are some fairly terrific buys at discount stores, where some wines go for as little as $3.99—a price level that seems all but dead elsewhere.

Cabernet Sauvignon

Cabernet is California's best red grape, produced in a broad range of styles, including deeply colored, rich, and tannic wines that are expensive and intended for long aging. In the under-$10 category, Cabernets tend to be less tannic and ready for drinking sooner. Of the 750 wineries in California, probably 75 to 80 percent make Cabernet Sauvignon, and there is enormous variation in quality and style. Consistently good ones like BV Beau Tour set a high standard, with good Cabernet character, firm structure, and smooth balance. Poorer wines of this category are blended with lesser grapes or made with Cabernet grown in hot, less desirable regions; they can be green, vegetal, or harsh. The list of good Cabernets, however, is fairly long. New ones continually come along, to which the better wine merchants should be able to alert you. But you can start with these.

Age: Best at 3–4 years, some will age 5–8 or longer
Price: $7–10
Recommended Producers:

Bandiera ✪
Bargetto Cypress
Beaulieu Beau Tour ✪
Beaulieu Rutherford ◆
Castoro Cellars
Christophe
Gran Val
Innisfree ◆
J. Lohr
Maddalena
Louis M. Martini ✪
The Monterey
  Vineyard Limited
  Release
Robert Mondavi
  Woodbridge
Meadow Glen
Michtom
J. W. Morris
Domaine St. George
Estancia ✪
Fetzer Lake County
Fetzer Barrel Select ✪
Foppiano
Golden Creek ✪
Pedroncelli
Poppy Hill
Rabbit Ridge
Raymond Cellars
Rolling Hills
Saddleback Cellars
Stratford ✱
J. Wile ✪
Whitehall Lane Le
  Petit
Willow Creek
Windsor Vineyards ✱

Foods: Beef, lamb, hamburgers, meat stews, pastas with meat sauce, cheeses mild and savory

Chardonnay

Chardonnay is California's top white grape, widely produced in styles that run the gamut from simple, fresh unoaked versions to rich, oaky, and powerful ones. There are some delightful inexpensive Chardonnays—lively, well balanced, and flavorful. As the category has exploded, however, there is a lot that is just plain lousy. It's shocking, in fact, what passes for Chardonnay today. I've already expressed my lament at the creeping sweetness enveloping Chardonnay, threatening to obliterate character altogether. Another thing to be wary of is inept winemaking (and not just at the inexpensive level). How do you avoid these? It is difficult because they are often heavily hyped. New names constantly appear in the fighting-varietal category. Few of them make my list—I want to see if they can prove themselves consistent. Some don't even make it out of the gate. If labels like Paraiso Springs and Montpellier want to make it, for instance, they should strive for a little more Chardonnay character in their wines. And don't come back at me with, "Well, what do you want for seven or eight dollars a bottle?" I want something *good*.

Since styles vary a bit, there are a couple of symbols that give a clue: ♥ indicates perceptible sweetness (but balanced with good crisp acidity); ■ represents little or no oak in the wine. Otherwise, they are perceptibly dry, with moderate oak.

Age: 1–2 years
Price: $6–10
Recommended Producers:

Alderbrook	Clos Robert ✪
Bandiera Carneros	Creston Manor
Belvedere Carneros	Domaine St. George
Black Mountain	Estancia ✪
Callaway Calla-Lees ♥ ■	Fetzer Barrel Select ◆
Canterbury ■	Fetzer Sundial ♥ ■
Chestnut Hill	Fremont Creek
Clos du Val Joli Val ✪	Glen Ellen

Proprietor's
Reserve ♥
Hawk Crest ✪
Hess Select ♦
Kendall-Jackson
Vintner's Reserve ♥ ✳
Konocti ■
La Petite Fleur
Leeward Bien Nacido ♦
J. Lohr Riverstone
McDowell ♥
Maddalena ✪
Masson Vineyards
Meadow Glen
The Monterey
Vineyard Classic ♥ ■

Mountain View
Parducci ■
Parson's Creek ♥
J. Pedroncelli
Christophe
Round Hill "House" ■
Round Hill Napa ✪
Seghesio ✪
Stratford ♦
Taft Street ✪
Weinstock ✪
Wente Monterey
Whitehall Lane Le
Petit
J. Wile
Zaca Mesa

Foods: Hard to match because styles differ; sweeter Chardonnays can handle chicken salad and other cold meats; drier ones with shellfish (especially shrimp), pastas with cream sauce, vegetables, or seafood; either can serve as aperitifs or summer-afternoon sippers

Chenin Blanc

Chenin Blanc is the grape that makes Vouvray and the excellent Savennières in the Loire Valley. California Chenin rarely achieves the character found in the best of those wines, but several producers are making good, fresh, stylish wines. A good many, however, are merely insipid. Two styles exist, dry or slightly off-dry, and lightly sweet, the latter redeemed by good acidity that makes for liveliness. Both are best when young and fresh, but we list them separately.

Age: 1–2 years
Price: $6.50–9.50

Recommended Producers:
   Dry. Chapellet ❍, Folie à Deux, Girard, Hacienda
   ❍, Kenwood, Preston ❍, Sullivan, Ventana
   Lightly Sweet. Callaway, Fetzer, Grand Cru, Rob-
   ert Mondavi, Parducci, Pedroncelli, Pine Ridge,
   Simi, Stevenot, Weibel
Foods: Dry with light fish, white meat chicken;
   sweet with chicken salad, ham, liver pâté

Gamay Beaujolais, Napa Gamay

Can America make a light, fruity red with the
charm of good Beaujolais? Some producers are
trying mightily, with round, fruity, quaffable
wines that are proving popular. Some vintners
haven't mastered the techniques, however; less
good versions can be thin and rather mean. The
good ones, like Beaujolais, are best within a
year or so of the vintage, and more appealing if
they are lightly chilled. The list below includes
nouveau.

Age: 6–18 months, maybe 2 years
Price: $5–8.50
Recommended Producers: Beringer, Castoro,
   Fetzer, Gan Eden, Glen Ellen ❍, Kendall-Jack-
   son, J. Lohr, Robert Pecota, Charles F. Shaw ❍,
   Weinstock ❍
Foods: Hamburgers, pizza, fried chicken, sausages,
   cold meats

Gewurztraminer

California Gewurztraminer is usually sweet,
with a hint of spiciness in aroma and flavor.
Even those labeled Dry tend to be off-dry, not
bone-dry like their counterparts in Alsace.
When acidity is high and the wines are crisp and

lively, they are delightful to drink and can be enjoyed on their own or with food, especially rich Oriental dishes that are deep-fried and some Thai dishes.

Age: 1–3 years
Price: $6.50–10
Recommended Producers: Beringer, Buena Vista, Clos du Bois Early Harvest (dry), Davis Bynum, De Loach, Fieldstone, Fetzer, Firestone, Gundlach-Bundschu (dry), Handley, Husch, Mark West, Navarro ✪, Pedroncelli, Joseph Phelps, Round Hill, Rutherford Hill (off-dry), St. Francis, Wente (dry)
Foods: Spicy and deep-fried Oriental foods, spicy chicken salad, fresh fruit or fruit salads; by itself

---

Merlot

Well-made Merlot no longer takes a backseat to Cabernet as one of California's best reds—it sits right there on the front seat. Some Merlots are as tough and firm as Cabernet when they're young, but the less expensive ones often accentuate the grape's soft, plummy fruit and alluring texture. They're mostly ready to drink when you buy them, and often your best match with lamb. If you buy one that seems a little tight, decant it out of and back into the bottle, which should aerate it enough to soften it. Very good Merlot is available for under $10, and outstanding ones for a few dollars more.

Age: Drinkable at 2 years, best at 3–4, can hold 5–7
Price: $7.50–10
Recommended Producers: Canterbury, Firestone ◆, Flora Springs Stray Cuvée, Geyser Peak, Glen Ellen, Golden Creek ✪, Guenoc, Inglenook Reserve, Lakespring, Markham, Louis M. Martini ◆,

Masson Vineyards, Meadow Glen, Monterey
Vineyard Classic, Mountain View, Parducci, Se-
bastiani, Trentadue
Foods: Lamb, roast beef, steak, duck, goose, rabbit,
grilled tuna

Muscat Canelli

Good Muscat, with its lightly spicy, faintly exotic flavors, is becoming more popular, happily.
It is lightly sweet unless the label says Late Harvest. My hope is that someone takes up the chal-
lenge to produce a fine *dry* Muscat that isn't
bitter—hard to do, so it may be a while. Meanwhile, there are some charming Muscats to sip
on a late sunny afternoon, or to enjoy with a
ripe peach.

Age: 1 year
Price: $7–8
Recommended Producers: Alderbrook, Eberle,
 Preston, Folie à Deux, Quady Electra
Foods: Peaches, pears, papayas, strawberries; by it-
 self

Petite Sirah, Syrah

Petite Sirah is an old variety in California, originally thought to be the Syrah of the Rhône Valley. Turns out it's a lesser variety known there
as the Durif, used primarily for blending. Petite
Sirah was once widely planted in warmer regions and used to beef up jug wines, but a few
producers produce dark, hefty, richly textured
reds from it that have flavors of black raspberries and some of the peppery character of
Rhône reds.

Syrah is the genuine Rhône variety used to
make some of the Rhône Valley's most distin-

guished reds, such as Hermitage, Côte Rotie, and Cornas. Syrah is still fairly new to California, but it's hot because several innovative winemakers have produced some dramatic reds with it. Limited in quantity, most Syrahs cost well over $10; those that don't tend to be lighter in character and pizzazz. Those included here are listed with the Petite Sirahs, but Syrah follows the winery name.

Age: **3–5 years, will age**
Price: **$5.50–9**
Recommended Producers: **Bogle, Foppiano, Guenoc, Louis M. Martini ✪, McDowell Les Vieux Cépages, Parducci, Joseph Phelps Syrah, Renaissance DaVinci, Rosenbloom, Trentadue**
Foods: **Grilled steak, braised brisket, meat or game stews, savory cheeses like aged Cheddar, Parmesan, or Asiago, dry Jack; also goat and blue cheeses**

Pinot Blanc

A firm, dry white, medium-bodied, often described as a leaner Chardonnay. Fruity and lightly oaked (occasionally barrel-fermented), Pinot Blanc is a good alternative to Chardonnay —more satisfying, in fact, than some of the bland, sweetish Chardonnays that seem to be proliferating. There aren't many Pinot Blancs, but some new planting is under way, so we may see more.

Age: **1–2 years, can stretch**
Price: **$8–10**
Recommended Producers: **Benziger, Buehler, Congress Springs, Jekel, Lockwood, Mirassou White Burgundy (mostly Pinot Blanc), Ventana**

Pinot Noir

California is producing some outstanding Pinot
Noirs these days, the best of them fairly pricey.
Good ones under $10 tend to be lighter, fruitier,
accessible at a younger age, and quite versatile
with a broad range of foods. If they are quite
light, the flavor may be enhanced by slight chilling, but it isn't necessarily color that tells you
that. Some of the cherry-colored Pinots have
quite intense flavor, without the tannin of their
more exalted brothers.

Age: 2–4 years
Price: $6–10
Recommended Producers: **Beaulieu Carneros, Con-
gress Springs ✪, Creston Manor Petit d'Noir,
Davis Bynum ✪, The Monterey Vineyard, Moun-
tain View ✪, Navarro, Saintsbury Garnet ✪,
Seghesio, Windsor Carneros**
Foods: **Grilled or roast chicken, duck, grilled
salmon, roast pork, country pâtés, mild cheeses
like Port Salut, Monterey Jack**

Pinot Noir Blanc

If you take red grapes and drain off the free-
run juice or press it lightly, you'll get wines
with a light blush color—deeper, if more time
with the grape skin is allowed, since that is
where the color pigments are. These can be
delightful wines when well made, perfect for
sipping or for weekend brunches or picnics.
They should be quite crisp and not too sweet,
like those recommended below. Most pink
wines today are made from Zinfandel, but a
few very good ones are still made from Pinot
Noir. They can sure cool down a chili-lacerated
palate.

Age: 6–18 months
Price: $4–8
Recommended Producers: Buena Vista Steelhead
    Run, Caymus Oeil de Perdrix, Hagafen, Leeward
    Coral, The Monterey Vineyard Classic
Foods: Ham, cold cuts, cold chicken or turkey,
    chicken salad, goat-cheese salad, spicy Mexican

Proprietary Reds

These blended reds are given simple names like
Red Table Wine or Vintage White, sometimes
proprietary names like Trefethen's Eshcol or
Boeger's whimsical Hangtown Red. They are
usually made from surplus varieties, often
grown on the estate, and can be excellent value
for everyday drinking—or even a bit better than
that. Most are light or medium-bodied, but
some, like Marty Griffin's Big Red, are robust
and meaty. Other good ones pop up from time
to time, but the ones listed here are consistently
good. Some come in 1.5-milliliter metric magnums (a liter and a half), a convenient size for
large gatherings. Also included is a lone varietal, the Martini Barbera (for lack of anywhere
else to put it).

Age: Often nonvintage, always ready for immediate
    drinking
Price: $4–7.50
Recommended Producers: Boeger Hangtown
    Red ✪, Bonny Doon Clos de Gilroy ✪, Domaine
    St. George Red, Fetzer Premium Red, Marty Grif-
    fin's Big Red ✪, Granval Red, Haywood Spaghetti
    Red, Heitz Ryan's Red, Le Clos Red, Louis M.
    Martini Barbera, Mendocino Timber Ridge Red,
    The Monterey Vineyards Classic Red, Pedron-
    celli Sonoma Red, R. H. Phillips Night Harvest

Cuvée Rouge ✪, Preston Estate Red, Raymond,
Trefethen Eshcol Red, Trentadue Red
Foods: Hamburgers to grilled steak

Proprietary Whites

The story is the same for proprietary whites—
the best are from estate surplus or carefully selected purchased grapes. Some could be labeled
with varietal names. Trefethen's outstanding
Eschol White contains 75 to 90 percent Chardonnay, for instance. Mirassou's White Burgundy is mostly Pinot Blanc. I prefer the drier
ones, but some are off-dry or lightly sweet and
also quite well made (sweetness noted by symbol). Merlion's Coeur de Melon is made from
the Melon grape that produces French Muscadet.

Age: Most are nonvintage, within a year for those
  vintage-dated.
Price: $4–6.50
Recommended Producers: Château St. Jean Vin
  Blanc ♥, Gran Val White, Handley Brightlighter
  White ♥, La Crema Crème de Tête ♥, Merlion
  Coeur de Melon, Mirassou White Burgundy, Par-
  ducci Vintage White ♥, Preston Estate White ♥,
  Trefethen Eschol White ✪.
Foods: Can accompany a broad range of casual
  foods; fine by themselves

Riesling (Johannisberg or White)

Riesling is such a hard sell in the United States
that many Riesling vineyards have been grafted
over to other varieties, mostly Chardonnay (the
easy sell). Some of the best producers are still
at it, happily, producing some very charming

wines. The true German Riesling is called Johannisberg or White Riesling in California to
distinguish it from lesser Riesling varieties (like
Franken Riesling or Monterey Riesling, which
are actually Sylvaner). Styles of Riesling range
from off-dry to lightly sweet to very sweet late-
harvest and Botrytised wines. Though the grape
does not achieve the depth and complexity that
it does at the great estates of the Rhine and
Mosel valleys in Germany, there are a number
of lovely, fragrant, flowery Rieslings made here,
and truly luscious late-harvest ones. Light Rieslings are never more than $10, and most are
well under that. However, only a few of the late-
harvest wines—that I can recommend, at any
rate—fall within our limits. Many of these
wines come in half-bottles. Rieslings are charming when they are young and fresh, but well-
balanced ones, dry or sweet, will keep several
years if properly stored in cool conditions. I
once tasted a ten-year-old Chappellet Dry Riesling that was as crisp and fresh as a two-year-
old one, and much more interesting. Like many
wineries, Chapellet stopped making Riesling
some years ago.

Wines labeled Dry Riesling are rarely com-
pletely dry here, but high acidity in the good
ones makes them seem quite dry. For clarity,
I've separated the three most popular styles in
our price range as follows: Dry, Lightly Sweet,
and Late Harvest.

Age: 1–3 years, Late Harvest can last 5–8 or more
   depending on balance
Price: $6–10
Dry, Off-dry: **Clos du Bois, Firestone, Greenwood
   Ridge ✪, Jekel, Konocti, Joseph Phelps, Renais-
   sance, Trefethen**

Foods: Chicken, chicken salad, Oriental foods, light fish such as sea bass, trout, pike; smoked salmon; good aperitif

Lightly Sweet: Babcock, Fetzer ✪, Firestone ✪, Freemark Abbey, Grgich Hills, Haywood , Hidden Cellars, Jekel ✪, Kendall-Jackson, Louis M. Martini, Masson Vineyards, Robert Mondavi, Obester, Parducci, St. Francis, Ventana, Wente, Zaca Mesa

Foods: Delightful on their own, with fresh fruit or light desserts; foods with sweet sauces

Late Harvest: Arciero, Franciscan, Kendall-Jackson, Pedroncelli, Rodney Strong LeBaron

Foods: Fruit desserts, particularly those made with peaches or apricots; can also serve *as* dessert, with light cake or cookies

Rosés

Rosés are slightly less in favor with the advancement of the popular blush, White Zinfandel. Generic rosés can be vapid and feeble. If you want rosé, varietal rosés, those made from a single variety such as Zinfandel or Cabernet Sauvignon, are the only way to go. I don't have many to recommend, but they are the best of the breed. Most are lightly sweet (the Firestone is the driest), but well balanced and crisp. See also Vin Gris.

Age: 1–2 years
Price: $5–7.50
Recommended: Firestone Rosé of Cabernet Sauvignon, Mirassou Petite Rosé, Robert Mondavi Woodbridge Gamay Rosé, Pedroncelli Zinfandel Rosé, Simi Rosé of Cabernet Sauvignon
Foods: Barbecues, picnics, Tex-Mex, dishes laced with chilis

Sauvignon Blanc (also labeled Fumé Blanc)

The runner-up in white wines, running a close second to inexpensive Chardonnays—and often surpassing them for my money. Dry, crisp, made with much greater finesse than formerly, Sauvignon Blancs represent some of the best values in California white wine. You never have to lay out more than $10 to get good, even excellent, Sauvignon Blanc—despite the fact that some of the front runners have become pretty pricey. It's not that they aren't worth it, it's just that there are so many good ones for less. It's the largest single category, in fact. The names Sauvignon Blanc and Fumé Blanc are used at the whim of the winery and are not a useful clue to style.

Styles do vary. Some are simple, made in a Loirelike style with no oak influence. More and more Sauvignons, however, are barrel-fermented or aged for a time in oak, which adds an extra dimension. Sémillon is sometimes blended with them. Styles from a given winery may change from one year to the next—no oak in one vintage, then a switch to oak aging or barrel fermentation the next. Most are dry, but some have residual sugar—I include only the well-made ones that are well balanced with acidity. Perceptible sweetness is indicated by the symbol ♥. The term Fumé is included when the wine is so-labeled; otherwise the label reads Sauvignon Blanc. Some wineries produce both, so the one that is recommended is indicated.

Age: 1–2 years, some go 3 or 4
Price: $7–10
Recommended Producers:

Adler Fels	Benziger Estate
Alderbrook	Sauvignon Blanc ♥

Beringer Knight's
  Valley Fumé
Brander ✪
J. Carey
Caymus
Chalk Hill
Château St. Jean
  Sonoma Fumé ♥
Concannon
DeLoach Fumé ♥
Dry Creek Fumé ✳ ♦
Ferrari-Carano ♥ ✳
Foppiano
Gallo ♥
Greenwood Ridge
Groth
Hanna
Hawk Crest ✪
Louis Honig
Husch ♥
Kendall-Jackson Clear
  Lake ♥
Kenwood
Konocti Fumé ✪
Markham

Louis M. Martini
Merlion Sauvrier
Robert Mondavi
  Fumé ✪
The Monterey
  Vineyard
Morgan Murphy-
  Goode Fumé ✪
Olson Fumé
Parducci
Pedroncelli Fumé
R. H. Phillips
Preston Cuvée de
  Fumé
Quivira
Round Hill House
  Fumé ✪
Sanford
Simi
Rodney Strong
  Charlotte's Home
  Vyd Fumé
Stonegate
Stratford

Vin Gris

I'm greatly in hopes this category will grow. Essentially, *vin gris* is a pale, *dry* rosé or blush wine made from red grapes. There are only a few made in California, hardly what you would call a category. American consumers are unfamiliar with the concept, expecting pink wines always to be sweet. Sanford Winery made an excellent dry *vin gris* from Pinot Noir for several years, then stopped because it didn't sell. I'm glad to report that as of 1989 Richard Sanford is making it again in small quantities. The

popularity of Bonny Doon's Vin Gris de Mourvèdre (a Rhône variety) is helping. I've urged
Au Bon Climat to have a go at *vin gris*—as long
as they keep it under $10. Maybe others will
follow suit. The important thing is that it be *dry;*
otherwise it is not a true *vin gris.*

Age: 1–2 years, sometimes 3
Price: $7–9
Recommended Producers: Sanford ✪, Bonny Doon
   Vin Gris de Mourvèdre ✪, Calera, Edna Valley,
   Saintsbury Vincent Vin Gris
Foods: Grilled sausages, prosciutto, roast ham or
   pork, cold chicken, smoked turkey, duck, goat
   cheese; alone, as an aperitif, or with snacks

Zinfandel

The most American of reds, generally robustly
fruity, with flavors reminiscent of raspberries or
huckleberries. Some versions are fairly tannic,
with chewy textures, but the tannic monsters of
yore have largely disappeared and certainly are
not recommended here. In fact, the bulk of Zinfandel grapes now go to make white Zinfandel,
diverting a lot of the mediocre wine that used to
be made by the tankful. The best practitioners
of Zinfandel continue to make rich, wonderful
reds that are excellent value, with a number of
Superbuys! Many good ones are priced at $10
and under. Some of the most sought-after are
made in limited quantities and can command
more; often they are worth it, though they are
sometimes found for less at discount stores. A
few good ones are made in a lighter style and
are so designated below. Zinfandel is prized for
its appealing thrust of fruit, showiest in its first
few years. But well-balanced Zinfandels (under

13.5 percent alcohol) can age a decade or more, becoming rather Cabernetlike with age.

Age: **Often drinkable at 2 years, but richer ones at 3–5; well-balanced Zins can age a decade or longer**
Price: **$7–10+**
Recommended Producers:

Buehler	Ravenswood Vintner's
Burgess	Reserve
Castoro ✪	Ridge Paso Robles ✹
Château Souverain	Ridge Sonoma ✹
Cline	Riverside Farm
Coturri	(light) ✪
Hop Kiln	Rosenblum ♦
Kendall-Jackson	Round Hill Napa
Mendocino	Select
Lamborn Family	Sarafornia
Louis M. Martini ✪	Sausal
Meeker	Storybook Mountain
Quivira ♦	✹ ♦
Pedroncelli	Sutter Home Reserve
Preston	V. Sattui
Rabbit Ridge	Villa Mt. Eden
A. Rafanelli ✪	

White Zinfandel

Just because most white Zinfandel is sweet and insipid doesn't mean there aren't truly charming ones that are only lightly sweet, crisp, lively and well balanced. These I can recommend happily for casual sipping.

Age: **6–18 months**
Price: **$5–6.50**
Recommended Producers: **Bandiera, Buehler, De-Loach ✪, Louis M. Martini ✪, Mirassou, Robert Mondavi Woodbridge ✪, The Monterey Vine-**

yard, Mountain View, Pedroncelli, Stevenot,
Weinstock

Other U.S. Wines

Wines from other parts of the United States are
steadily improving. Some, indeed, have arrived,
especially those of the Northwest, which is producing wines that can rival many of the best
from California (Riesling, Sauvignon Blanc,
Cabernet, Pinot Noir). Washington and Oregon wines are also gaining wider distribution
around the country, as future editions of this
book will undoubtedly reflect. The same is true
for New York, where the small wineries have
effected a dramatic revolution in quality and
style. Texas and Virginia are also growing rapidly and producing excellent wines.

Many of the best regional wines have escalated in price as their quality has gained recognition. However, those that fall within our price
range are well worth seeking out if you find
yourself in their immediate areas.

Arkansas. Wiederkehr Cabernet Sauvignon,
     Vidal, Johannisberg Riesling
Colorado. Plum Creek Cellars Merlot
Connecticut. Crosswoods Scrimshaw White,
     Chardonnay
     Chambord Chardonnay
Idaho. Ste. Chapelle Riesling
Maryland. Catoctin Chardonnay
     Boordy White
Michigan. Château Grand Traverse Riesling
     Fenn Valley Chancellor
Missouri. Les Bourgeois Vidal
     Mt. Pleasant Vidal, Vintage Port
     Stone Hill Norton

New Jersey. Alba Riesling, Vidal Reserve
    Tewksberry Gewurztraminer
New Mexico. Gruet Brut
    La Chiripada Primavera
New York. Banfi Old Brookville Chardonnay
   Bedell Cabernet Sauvignon, Chardonnay
   Glenora Chardonnay, Riesling
   Great Western Ice Wine
   Hargrave Petite Chardonnay, Petite
    Cabernet, Blanc de Pinot Noir
   Hermann Wiemer Dry Riesling
   Konstantin Frank Johannisberg Riesling
   Lenz Gewurztraminer
   Millbrook Chardonnay, Pinot Noir, Merlot
   Palmer Chardonnay
   Peconic Bay Chardonnay
   Pindar Merlot
   Wagner Seyval Blanc
   West Park Chardonnay
North Carolina. Biltmore Pinot Noir, Blanc de
    Blancs
Oregon. Oregon's best wines are Pinot Noir,
    but few fall within our price range.
    Riesling and Pinot Gris are often quite
    good.
   Adelsheim Pinot Gris
   Amity Riesling
   Bethel Heights Pinot Noir First Release
   Elk Cove Riesling
   Knudsen-Erath Pinot Noir ($10+)
   Ponzi Pinot Gris, Riesling
   Silver Falls Pinot Gris
   Tualatin White Riesling
   Tucker Gewurztraminer
Pennsylvania. Chaddsford Spring Wine,
    Nouveau
Texas. Domaine Cordier Chardonnay, Fumé
   Blanc

Fall Creek Emerald Riesling, Sauvignon
   Blanc, Cabernet Sauvignon, Red Table
   Wine
Llano Estacado Gewurztraminer, Riesling
Slaughter-Leftwych Sauvignon Blanc, Austin
   Blush
Teysha Gewurztraminer, Muscat Canelli
Virginia. Ingleside Plantation Chesapeake
   White, Blanc de Blancs, Cabernet
   Sauvignon
Meredyth Seyval Blanc, Chardonnay
Montdomaine Merlot ◆
Oakencroft Dry Seyval Blanc, Chardonnay
Prince Michel Blanc de Noir
Rapidan River Riesling
Williamsburg Chardonnay, St. James White
Washington. Arbor Crest Merlot, Sauvignon
   Blanc
Château Ste. Michelle Chardonnay,
   Sémillon, Cabernet Sauvignon
Columbia Gewurztraminer, Sémillon,
   Merlot, Johannisberg Riesling
Columbia Crest Merlot, Chardonnay
Covey Run Merlot, Chenin Blanc
Hogue Cellars Fumé Blanc, Merlot, Dry
   Reisling
Pacifica Dry White
Salishan Dry Riesling
Snoqualmie Chenin Blanc
Woodward Canyon Cabernet Sauvignon ◆
West Virginia. Robert Pliska Foch
Wisconsin. Wollersheim Reserve Red

SUPERBUYS / CALIFORNIA

White
   Estancia Chardonnay, $8–9
   Hawk Crest Chardonnay, $8

Round Hill Napa Chardonnay, $9
Seghesio Chardonnay, $7.50
Taft Street Chardonnay, $8
Trefethen Eschol White, $7.50
Kendall-Jackson Vintners' Reserve, $9.99 ✳
Weinstock Chardonnay (kosher), $7.50
Hacienda Chenin Blanc, $6.50
Chappellet Chenin Blanc, $8.50
Navarro Gewurztraminer, $8
Firestone Johannisberg Riesling, $8.50
Jekel Dry Riesling, $7.50
Grgich Hills Johannisberg Riesling, $8
Greenwood Ridge Dry Riesling, $8.50
Brander Sauvignon Blanc, $8
J. Carey Sauvignon Blanc, $9
Murphy-Goode Fumé Blanc, $8.50
Konocti Fumé Blanc, $7.50
Round Hill "House" Fumé Blanc, $5.50

Red
Bandiera Cabernet Sauvignon, $6.50
Beaulieu Cabernet Sauvignon Beau Tour, $6–8
J. Wile Cabernet Sauvignon, $7.99
Golden Creek Cabernet Sauvignon, $7.50
Golden Creek Merlot, $7.50
Estancia Cabernet Sauvignon, $7
Bonny Doon Clos de Gilroy, $7.50
Gamay Beaujolais (Glen Ellen, Charles F. Shaw, Weinstock), $5–6.50
Louis M. Martini Petite Sirah, $7.50
Louis M. Martini Zinfandel, $8
Congress Springs Pinot Noir, $8.99
Davis Bynum Pinot Noir, $7.50
Saintsbury Garnet Pinot Noir, $9.99
Marty Griffin's Big Red, $5.99
R. H. Phillips Night Harvest Cuvée Rouge, $4.99
Boeger Hangtown Red, $4.50
Sanford Vin Gris, $7.50–8.95
Bonny Doon Vin Gris de Mourvèdre, $9.99
Zinfandel (Rafanelli, Castoro, Louis M. Martini, Quivira), $8–10

Latin America

Latin American wines are apt to emerge impressively during this decade. Chile has already made a big splash, producing sensational values in red wines (watch for Superbuys). Indeed, they compete favorably with red wines made anywhere now. Chile makes some remarkably flavorful and well-balanced Cabernet Sauvignon, Bordeauxlike in structure and style. This is not mere coincidence. When the terrible phylloxera (a bug that eats vine roots) devastated the vineyards of Bordeaux in the 1880s, several Bordeaux vintners came to Chile to make wine, establishing a style with Cabernet that is still followed today. Interest from Bordeaux also continues. Consulting enologist Emile Peynaud has lent his expertise to Chilean winemakers. The owners of Château Lafite-Rothschild have invested in vineyards there, producing wine under the Los Vascos label.

Several California vintners are also importing Chilean varietals.

Chilean Cabernets tend to be drinkable early but often have amazing capacity for aging many years. The climate and soils of Chile's inland valleys give the wines their edge in character and quality. In recent years, good Merlot, Sauvignon Blanc, and Chardonnay have also begun to appear. A problem for Chile is that, because the wines are so reasonable, many people have jumped on the bandwagon to bring in Chilean wines. Individuals go down from California, for instance, and buy up available wine, slap a label on it, and import it, hoping it will become a hot new property. Those who produce the best wines, though, are mostly well-established producers who have good vineyards, or newcomers who have bought or planted vineyards in the better regions. Chile is hot, and getting hotter.

The same cannot be said for Argentina. This country's wine potential has never been properly realized, merely exploited to produce as much quantity as possible with little regard to quality. Argentina is a sleeping giant, however; it could do more and better—if only Argentine vintners would begin to produce wines from lower yields with more concentration. The Argentine wine industry hasn't the global outlook that Chile has, and seems to have little sense of international standards. They produce as much as possible from every vineyard, extracting high yields that dilute character and make for mediocre quality. They age the wines in huge old wooden vats that do little to improve them (in fact, they may have the opposite effect) or in large stainless steel vats that contribute nothing to flavor—which would be all right except there is so little in the first place.

There are a few producers who do a good job, but by far the largest number are interested in quantity over quality. Argentine wines are grown on broad, flat plateaus in the northwestern part of the country at the foot of the Andes. The vines are grafted because phylloxera came in the late eighteenth century (The little bug did not cross the Andes, however, so Chilean vines grow on their own roots, accounting for some of the rather aggressive character when the vines are young.) Argentina is the fifth-largest producer of wine in the world and third in per capita consumption. Most of the wine stays in Argentina or goes elsewhere in South America. If Argentina ever awakes to what is possible, we may see excellent values here. As it is, I have only a few labels to recommend.

Mexico is another area of great potential, but here too they need to get their act together. At the moment the largest area for serious grape-growing is in Baja California, but vineyards in the central highlands have produced good Cabernet Sauvignon and other reds (including Zinfandel), as well as Chardonnay and Pinot Noir that offer positive hope for the future. Mexican wines got a boost when a Domecq Cabernet won recognition in the Paris Olympiad held by Gault-Millau.

Brazil and Uruguay also produce wine, and might possibly do well if the industry concentrates on clean, well-balanced wines. At the moment almost nothing is available here except the Marcus James label from Brazil, producing decent if unremarkable white Zinfandel and other inexpensive varietals.

CHILE

We would have been drinking the fine wines of Chile far sooner had it not been for a political climate that interfered with exports. Since the early 1980s, however, the wines have flowed north in greater number, and Americans have been pleased by the values they offer, particularly in red wines.

Chile's wine regions are in the inland valleys north and south of Santiago. Aconcagua is to the north, Maipo in the south with its subdistricts of Maule, Mataquito, Curicó, and Lontué. Though you will see such names on labels, at this stage the best guide to quality is the producer name.

In view of the growing quality and reputation of Chilean wines, we can expect to see prices rise for the better and more sought-after wines. It is rather amazing that one can purchase outstanding Cabernet Sauvignon such as the Cousiño Macul for as little as $6, and well under $10 for the Reserva. At their best, these wines are brimming with berryish fruit and cedary flavors typical of fine cabernet, but the good ones are never heavy or overripe.

Because of fine balance and medium body, Chilean Cabernet is remarkably versatile with food, from barbecued meats to roast chicken, lamb, or beef, as well as veal and light game, and savory cheese. Vintages are fairly even in Chile; poor vintages are rare; poorly made wines, however, are not so rare, a situation also likely to improve.

Chile now produces several other varietals, such as Merlot, and Pinot Noir in reds, Chardonnay, Sauvignon Blanc, Sémillon, and Riesling in whites. Sauvignon Blanc, dry, crisp, and rather steely, is the most successful other than Cabernet at the moment. The others I would rate average to good, but future prospects as the vines mature and winemakers gain experience with Merlot, Pinot Noir, and Chardonnay look bright.

Best Wine:
   Cabernet Sauvignon
Next:
   Sauvignon Blanc
   Merlot
   Chardonnay

Cabernet Sauvignon

There are some sensational values here, and the better properties rarely miss, though on occasion a few of the regular Cabernets (non-Reservas) taste a little thin. Cousiño Macul, for instance, consistently scores with simple Cabernet, but the 1986 was exaggeratedly vegetal—perhaps due to wines from young vines. The Santa Rita 120, on the other hand, is quite jammy, somewhat on the mellow side, while Concha y Toro Cabernets tend to be coarse and rustic. The best values by far are the Reservas. These are better lots of wine that are aged longer and have the most flavor and depth. Cousiño Macul's Antiguas Reserva is outstanding, as are the Reservas of Santa Rita, Errazuriz Panquehue, and Concha y Toro Casillero del Diablo. These wines, smooth and ready to drink when you buy them, nevertheless have the balance and depth to age further, easily to eight or ten years. New labels are rapidly appearing from Chile, some good, some not.

Age: 2–4 years; Reservas 4–6, may go 8–10 or
   more
Price: $4.50–6; Reservas $6–10
Recommended Producers: Canepa Finisimo, Cali-
   terra ✪, Casillero del Diablo, Cousiño Macul
   (Antiguas Reserva) ✳, Errazuriz Panquehue, Los
   Vascos ✪ (Reserva ✪), Miguel Torres, Santa Rita
   Medalla Real ✪, Santa Carolina (Reserva ✪),
   Saint Morillon, Undurraga
Foods: Reservas are excellent with lamb or beef,
   grilled or roasted; non-Reservas with lighter
   fare, like hamburgers, grilled chicken, veal stew

Chardonnay

Chile is just getting started with Chardonnay,
and plantings are expanding rapidly. Some of
the wines are fresh and attractive but don't
have much character yet; that should come as
the vines mature. While at the moment Sauvignon Blanc is a better buy, I believe the Chardonnays of Chile will come into their own, and
they bear watching. Don't look for rich, oaky
styles yet (which will likely cost more anyway)
—the wines are dry, fruity, simple but increasingly appealing. Chardonnay grapes seem to
cost more everywhere, and prices for some Chilean Chardonnay are at the upper end of the
scale.

Age: 1–3 years
Price: $5–8
Recommended Producers: Caliterra ✳, Casillero
   del Diablo, Cousiño Macul, Los Vascos, Miguel
   Torres, Santa Rita Reserva, Valdivieso
Foods: Simply prepared fish, cold shrimp, chicken
   (white meat), smoked turkey

Merlot

Not as widely planted as Cabernet Sauvignon, and the wines are not as impressive as yet. More vineyards are being planted, and there is every reason to expect Merlot to do well in Chile as winemakers become more experienced with the variety. Good ones have plummy, berryish fruit, but some of the wines have a vegetal accent that should be toned down (or, one hopes, eliminated altogether); others seem overchaptalized (sugar added before fermentation to add body)—hence, the few recommendations that appear here.

Age: 2–4 years
Price: $4–6
Recommended Producers: Concha y Toro, Gato de Oro, Santa Rita, Errazuriz
Foods: Burgers, pork chops, quiche, and other cheese dishes

Sauvignon Blanc

Chilean winemakers are old hands with Sauvignon Blanc, and it is their finest white wine at the moment. Top ones are dry, crisp, and snappy, though sometimes the tartness and sharp angularity of young Sauvignons bites a bit (especially in those for under $4.50). Reservas have more flavor and better balance. Los Vascos makes one of the cleanest, smoothest, and most appealing Sauvignons—an excellent example of what can be done when the grapes are balanced and the winemaking is skilled and conscientious.

Age: 1–3 years
Price: $4.50–7
Recommended Producers: Caliterra ✴, Cousiño
   Macul, Errazuriz Panquehue ✴, Los Vascos Re-
   serva ⊙, Marqués de Casa, Miguel Torres ⊙,
   Santa Rita Reserva, Saint Morillon, San Pedro
Foods: Shellfish, swordfish, shark, roasted red
   peppers with garlic, goat cheese, seafood
   pastas

SUPERBUYS / CHILE

White
   Caliterra Chardonnay, $7
   Canepa Sauvignon Blanc, $5.99
   Los Vascos Sauvignon Blanc, $5.99

Red
   Canepa Cabernet Sauvignon, $7
   Cousiño Macul Cabernet Sauvignon Antiguas
      Reservas, $7.50–9
   Los Vascos Cabernet Sauvignon, $5.99
   Errazuriz Panquehue Cabernet Sauvignon, $7
   Santa Rita Medalla Real, $7.49–8
   Santa Carolina Cabernet Reserva, $8

ARGENTINA

Argentina should be producing good, sturdy, flavorful reds and crisp stylish whites. Surely vintners will get the message sometime during this
decade and begin to produce wines that are
worthy of attention, and the consumer's dollar.
Meanwhile, precious little that can meet those
demands is available in the United States as yet.
Of those imported, Cabernet Sauvignon is the

best, but other varietals with promise are Syrah
(Navarro Correas), Merlot, Riesling, and Chardonnay.

Cabernet Sauvignon

Cabernet is often blended with Malbec, a lesser
Bordeaux red grape, and some Merlot, though
little is grown there as yet. Most Argentine Cabernet is medium weight in terms of body, without much structure or depth, but some of the
meatier ones are quite good.

Age: 3–6 years
Price: $6–7
Recommended Producers: Bianchi Particular, Na-
   varro Correas ✳, Pascual Toso, San Felipe, Trap-
   iche
Foods: Steak, roast beef, beef stew, grilled chicken

Chardonnay

There is not a lot of varietal character in Argentine Chardonnays, but they do have freshness
and a crisp, stylish appeal that shows what Argentine wineries can do with the grape when
they try. The ones recommended are quite reasonable and well worth a try; others may soon
surface.

Age: 1–2 years
Price: $5–8
Recommended Producers: Navarro Correas, San
   Felipe, Trapiche
Foods: Mild fish or chicken, scallops

Syrah

Syrah could prove to be one of Argentina's finest reds. The climate is highly suitable to this Rhône variety. Most is rather light in style now, but watch for sturdier versions to make their appearance in the next few years.

Age: 2–5 years
Price: $8–10
Recommended Producer: Navarro Correas
Foods: Burgers, chops, grilled sausage

Germany

The nineties, I believe, will bring much greater
acceptance of German wines—and deservedly.
Germany makes some of the most delectable
wines available, but for too long they have been
outré—out, because dry wines are "in" and
German wines are sweet. There ought to be
room for both styles; they are not exactly interchangeable. With some foods only dry will do,
but there are times when off-dry or lightly
sweet is perfection. Try a Kabinett Riesling with
smoked salmon to see what I mean; Chardonnay just can't handle it. Novice wine drinkers
who prefer sweet wines can do no better than
hone their palates on fine Rieslings from the
Rhine and Mosel valleys.

Most of the people who avoid German Rieslings either have never tasted them, or have
tasted poor ones. Pour a good one, however,
and it isn't hard to win someone over. They are
easy wines to like. The worldwide demand for

dry wine hurt German wine sales during the
eighties. As a result, drier styles of German
wine (Trocken and Halbtrocken) have emerged.
Some, especially those labeled Halbtrocken Kabinett or Spätlese, are very exciting wines with
some outstanding values among them.

Another reason people ignore German wines
is that they seem too difficult to understand—
those Gothic labels are beautiful but hard to
read, and many of the terms are unpronounce-
able if you don't know German. Don't let that
put you off—the wine inside those tall green
(Mosel) or brown (Rhine) bottles is light, fruity,
friendly, and delicious, frequently compelling in
character but never forbidding. I won't try to
explain German geography and nomenclature
here. There are several current books that do a
good job of that, so seek them out if you want
to know more.

Here I *am* going to define certain terms to
look for on the label and name some of the top
estates, producers, and importers of reliable
quality with fairly reasonable distribution
across the country.

Riesling. This is Germany's finest wine grape,
the only grape that consistently produces well
in Germany. If the label does not specifically say
Riesling, then some other grape variety (Müller-
Thurgau, Kerner, Sylvaner) is used, and none
compare in character, flavor, or quality. You
won't see Riesling on Liebfraumilch; by German
law the wine must contain only 51 percent Riesling, and rarely contains more. U.S. law re-
quires 75 percent for the grape to be named.
(Exceptions: Baden, which produces dry and
quite good Pinot Blanc (Weissburgunder), and
Pinot Gris (Rulander), as well as Riesling.

Trocken, Halbtrocken. Terms mean "dry" or "half-dry." Acidity in German Rieslings is high, so half-dry really comes across as quite dry.

Qualitätswein (QbA). The term means "quality wine," but it's the level for average to good wines.

Prädikat, or Qualitätswein mit Prädikat (QmP). The highest quality level for German wines, those with only natural sweetness. This level is further divided into five levels that indicate degrees of sweetness, as follows:

Kabinett. The driest level of Prädikat wines, but often off-dry or faintly sweet. It can be excellent value at $7 to $9. Kabinett Halbtrocken tends to be firmly dry.

Spätlese. Means "late harvest" and signifies richer wines than Kabinett but still only lightly sweet, especially those labeled Halbtrocken.

Auslese. "Specially selected late harvest," definitely sweet and quite luscious, the grapes often affected by the noble rot *Botrytis cinerea (Edelfäule* in German), the same mold that creates Sauternes. The best are too expensive for us, but check out specials or discount stores, which may have them marked down.

Beerenauslese (BA), Trockenbeerenauslese (TBA), and Eiswein. Germany's sweetest nectars, concentrated knockouts but limited in quantity, and very expensive, even in half-bottles.

Prices for Kabinetts and Spätlesen have already begun to rise from the top estates. Until the momentum for fine German wines gathers steam, however, you will find many of them marked down. Listed below are the top producers and estates, as well as shippers or importers who are reliable. It is interesting to note that producers committed to quality usually demonstrate excellent quality at all levels of production, from simple QbA Rieslings to their finest Auslesen.

CAUTION: *Beware* really cheap prices of $5 or under unless you personally know the wine and like it, or it is one listed here that's on sale or discounted. Wines of those marked ♦, unfortunately, rarely fall within our price limit but can be well worth a few extra dollars.

Top producers

Mosel
Bergweiler-Prüm
J. J. Christoffel
Conrad-Bartz
Deinhard
Friedrich-Wilhelm
   Gymnasium
Dr. Fischer
Fritz Haag
Willi Haag
H. Kerpen
von Kesselstatt
Maximin Grünhof
Maximinhof
Merkelbach
Meulenhof
Mönchhof
Moselland-
   Zentrallkererei
Egon Müller ♦

Pauly-Bergweiler
J. J. Prüm ♦
Max Richter
Willi Schäfer
Wolfgang Schwaab
Selbach-Oster
Dr. H. Thanisch ♦
Vereinigte Hospitien
von Hovel
von Voxelm
von Schleinitz
Wegeler-Deinhard
F. Weins-Prüm

Rhine
Balbach Erben
Bassermann-Jordan
H. Braun
von Brentano
von Buhl

Burklin-Wolf
Crusius (Nahe) ◆
Diefenhardt
H. Dönnhoff (Nahe)
Müller-Catoir ◆
Schumann Nagler
Petri-Essling (Nahe)
Balthasar Ress
Schloss Johannisberg
Schloss Eltz
Jacob Schneider

Schloss Schönborn
Schloss
  Reinhartshausen
Schloss Vollrads ◆
Reinhold Senfter
von Simmern
Staatsweingut Eltville
J & H Strub
Domdechant Werner
Fischer Erben
Siegfried Gerhard

Reliable Shippers and Importers

These names on German wines consistently indicate quality:

A Terry Theise Estate
  Selection
Deinhard

H. Sichel Söhne
Scholl & Hillebrand

Selected Villages and Vineyards
of Superior Quality

NOTE: Villages always have "er" attached to village name. The names following the village are
vineyard, *Einzellage,* or a collective of superior
vineyards *(Grosslage).* Best buys in brackets
from certain producers.

Ayler: Kupp [Gebrüder Kramp]
Bad Kreuznacher: Brückes, Kahlenberg, Stein-
  weg [Krönenberg]
Bernkasteler: Bereich [Sichel]
Bernkasteler: (Badstube Kurfürstlay) [Wegeler-
  Deinhard ✪, Weins-Prüm, Selbach-Oster,
  Friedrich Wilhelm, Vereinigte Hospitien,
  Prüm, Sichel, Terry Theise Selection, Berg-
  weiler-Prüm]

Brauneberger: Juffer [F. Haag ✪, von Kesselstatt, Richter]

Deidesheimer: Herrgottsacker, Leinhöhle, Ho-
henmorgen (Mariengarten) [Bassermann-
Jordan, Bürklin-Wolf, von Buhl]

Eltviller: Sonnenberg, Taubenberg [Staats-
weingut, von Simmern]

Erbacher: Marcobrunn ♦ [von Schönborn, Rein-
hartshausen]

Erdener: Treppchen [W. Schwaab, Meulenhof,
Mönchhof, Bergweiler-Prüm, Christoffel]

Forster: Jesuitengarten, Kirchenstück [Basser-
mann-Jordan, Bürklin-Wolf, Deinhard]

Geisenheim: Rothenberg, Mönchspad (Burgweg) [Deinhard, Zweirlein]

Graacher: Himmelreich, Josephshöfer ✪ [Tha-
nisch Spätlese, W. Schäfer Kabinett, von Kesselstatt Kabinett ✪]

Hallgartener: Jungfer [Deinhard, Eser, Siegfried
Gerhard Kabinett]

Haardter: [Müller-Catoir]

Hattenheimer: Steinberg, Nussbrunnen [B. Ress
Kabinett, S. Gerhard]

Hochheimer: Domdechaney, Kirchenstück [Dein-
hard, Ress, Schönborn]

Iphofener Franconia: Julius-Echter-Berg [Hans
Wirsching]

Johannisberger: Schloss Johannisberg [von Met-
ternich]

Maximin Grünhauser: Herrenberg [von Schu-
bert Kabinett]

Monzinger: [Petri-Essling]

Niederhauser: Hermannshöhle [Staatsweingut,
J. Schneider]

Niersteiner: Hipping, Olberg [Deinhard, R. Senfter, Strub]

Ockfener: Bockstein, Herrenberg [Deinhard
Spätlese ✪, Dr. Fischer]

Oppenheimer: Sackträger (Guldenmorgen)

Piesporter: Goldtröpfchen, Falkenberg, Hofber-
ger [Deinhard, von Kesselstatt Kabinett, Milz
Kabinett, Moselland]

Rauenthaler: Baiken, Gehrn, Wulfen [Staat-
sweingut, Diefenhardt]

Rüdesheimer: Berg (Burgweg) [Schloss Groen-
steyn, Scholl & Hillebrand]

Ruppertsberger: Reiterpfad [Bassermann-Jor-
dan, Bürklin-Wolf, von Buhl

Scharzhofberger: [von Kesselstatt, Egon Müller ◆]

Schlossböckelheimer: Kupfergrube, Felsenberg

Urziger: Wurzgarten [Mönchhof, Christoffel,
Merkelbach]

Wachenheimer: Gerümpel, Rechbächel [Bürk-
lin-Wolf]

Wehlener: Sonnenuhr [Deinhard, Kerpen, von
Kesselstatt, Moselland, Rudolf Müller, J. J.
Prüm ◆]

Wiltinger: Braune, Kupp, Klosterberg

Winkeler: Hasensprüng, Jesuitengarten [Ress,
Schönborn, Schloss Vollrads ◆, Wegeler-
Deinhard]

Zeltinger: Himmelreich [Friedrich Wilhelm,
Selbach-Oster]

Labels to Be Wary of Because
of Quality Variation (exceptions are
recommended shippers or importers)

Bereich Bernkasteler
Liebfraumilch (except Blue Nun, Hans
Christoffel)
Niersteiner Gutes Domtal
Piesporter Michelsberg
Piesporter Treppchen
Zeller Schwarze Katz

SUPERBUYS / GERMANY

Graacher Josefshoffer Riesling Kabinett, von
   Kesselstatt, $8.50

Brauneberger Juffer Riesling Kabinett, Willi
   Haag, $8.99

Dienheimer Falkenberg Riesling Kabinett, Dr.
   Becker, $8

Erdener Treppchen, Meulenhof, $8

Ockfener Bockstein Riesling Spätlese, Dr.
   Fischer, $8.99

Rheingau Bereich Johannisberg Riesling, Sichel,
   $6.29

Bernkasteler Badstube Riesling Kabinett,
   Wegeler-Deinhard, $9.50; Selbach-Oster
   Kabinett, $8

Niersteiner Hipping Spätlese, Strub, $10

Deinhard Riesling QbA, $7

Zeltinger Himmelreich Halbtrocken, $8

Monzinger Frühlingsplätzchen Riesling Kabinett,
   Petri-Essling, $8.99

Uerziger Wurzgarten, Christoffel, $9

Wehlener Sonnenuhr Kabinett, H. Kerpen, $8

Australia

When Australian wines hit the U.S. market a few years ago, their bold, vivid flavors made a big impact on American wine drinkers. Full-bodied Chardonnays with lots of oak and flamboyant fruit won many fans, as did the dark, berryish reds known as Shiraz. Some Cabernet Sauvignons were leaner, a little harder to like, but for the price—mostly $5 to $8 or $10 a bottle—Americans were more than willing to experiment with wines from Down Under.

At that time the exchange rate for the Australian dollar was more favorable than now. Though a few wines from small Australian wineries were available, most of the wine shipped at that stage was from large wineries and moderately priced. Now the situation has changed somewhat. Australia's stronger currency has boosted prices, and American enthusiasm for Aussie wines encouraged exports of more expensive ones. Good buys under $10 are somewhat scarcer as a result of these factors, but some real bargains remain. American consumers have shown some resistance, in fact, to higher prices, so that quite a few wines just over the limit can be found marked down (♦).

Australia's wine industry goes back some two hundred years, about the same time, give or take a few decades, that other New World wine regions (America, Chile, Argentina) were getting under way. As in those regions, it is the last two decades that have made all the difference in quality and style. Fast-growing and dynamic, the Australian wine industry now has some five hundred wineries, scattered across the southern half of the vast continent. There are many important growing regions—Hunter Valley, Barossa Valley, the Southern Vales, Coonawarra, Margaret River, and dozens more emerging into prominence.

Regions, however, are somewhat less important than varietal name and producer at this point—for American wine drinkers, at any rate. As in the California section, the wines are covered alphabetically by varietal, with a separate category for proprietary brands as well as for fortified and dessert wines. I have found that quality varies quite a bit with Australian wines, some of it due to still-evolving techniques in winemaking. Many of the large wineries have swallowed up smaller ones, and transitions in styles are still somewhat in flux. Only those wines that I have found to be consistently good are included here, but Australian exports have jumped tenfold in the last decade and continue to increase. As new labels appear, many of them may be well worth exploring, but it will be wise to exercise caution.

Cabernet Sauvignon

Cabernet is widely grown in Australia, ranging in style from wines that are rather firm, lean, and peppery in character to the richer, more intense versions flavored with essence of blackberry, cassis, and a good wallop of new oak. The costlier ones invariably need a few years of aging, as do the lean styles from the cool district of Coonawarra at the southern tip of South Australia. Less expensive Cabernets, usually intended for earlier drinking, are fruity and smooth, but on the whole Australian Cabernet is somewhat less generous than Shiraz, as well as more variable from vintage to vintage.

Age: Best at 3–5 years; sturdy ones can go 6, 8, even 10
Price: $7–10
Recommended Producers: Black Opal ◐, Brown Brothers Family Reserve ♦ ✳, Château Tahbilk, Peter Lehmann ◐, Lindemans Bin 45, Mildara Coonawarra ◐, Rosemount Diamond, St. Hugo, Seaview, Seppelt, Taltarni, Wirra Wirra McLaren Vale, Wolf Blass
Foods: Roast or grilled lamb and beef

Cabernet/Shiraz or Shiraz/Cabernet

Shiraz is the name for the Syrah grape in Australia, which produces robust, berryish reds (see Shiraz). The blend of Cabernet Sauvignon and Shiraz yields Australia's most popular red wine, sort of the Zinfandel of Australia, usually moderately priced and widely used as a hearty pour for casual or everyday use. Some of these wines are wonderfully fruity and flavorful, especially those that are predominantly Shiraz, such as Penfolds Koonunga Hill Shiraz/Cabernet, a Superbuy, you will note. Usually the varietal that is first dominates in the blend. Some, however, are labeled with proprietary names, such as Rosemount's Diamond Reserve Red, which is roughly half and half and an excellent value (see Proprietary Blends). Other grapes, such as Malbec and Merlot, may also be included in the blend and mentioned on the label.

Age: Drinkable on release, or within 2–4 years; some are nonvintage
Price: $7–10
Recommended Producers: Balgownie, Jacob's Creek, Mitchelton, Penfolds Koonunga Hill ☻, Seppelt, Wirra Wirra Church Block ♦, Wolf Blass, Wynn's Cabernet/Hermitage
Foods: Hearty barbecues, meat or game stews, goat cheese

Chardonnay

Australian Chardonnays fairly burst with flavor, with showy fruit that speaks of citrus or pineapple, spices like clove, cinnamon, and vanilla, and the rich, buttery character that comes from time in new oak barrels. This rush of flavor quite captivated American wine drinkers, especially when some of the top wines were going for $7 or $8 a bottle. That couldn't last forever, and didn't. Many of those Chardonnays now cost upward of $12. A number of wineries produce Chardonnays in various price categories. Quality variation at the under-$10 level is considerable, and many of these wines are too sweet for my taste. The better ones, however, are well balanced with rich, opulent flavors that many Chardonnay lovers find irresistible. Be on

the lookout for wines that are often marked
down (♦). Perceptible sweetness is noted by
the symbol ♥.

Age: 1–3 years
Price: $6.50–10+
Recommended Producers: Angove's, Black Opal ♥,
   Brown Brothers E.B. ✳, Château Reynella ♦ ✺,
   Hardy (Bird Series), Lindemans Bin 65 ♥, Mont-
   rose, Rosemount Diamond Label, Rothbury Es-
   tate Brokenback ♦, Seaview, Seppelt Reserve
   Bins ✺, Yeringberg Lilydale ✳ ♦
Foods: Can be overpowering with delicate or subtle
   foods, fine with spicy shellfish or grilled shrimp;
   less assertive ones go with fish, chicken, and pas-
   tas in cream sauce, wild mushrooms

Fumé Blanc, Sauvignon Blanc

As in California, the names are interchangeable
for wines made from the Sauvignon Blanc
grape. Australian Fumés are crisp and grassy,
with citrusy flavors of lime more than lemon,
perhaps because they all tend to be slightly
sweet. Cold fermentation and high acidity give
them lots of zing, though some are aggressively
herbacious and these are usually the ones that
are sweetened a bit to modify sharpness and
austerity.

New Zealand is coming on very strong with
Sauvignon Blanc, from areas like Hawkes Bay
and Marlborough. New Zealand Sauvignons
tend to be pricey, however, except for a couple
listed here (whose price tags are also inching
up). New Zealand wines are followed by NZ in
parenthesis.

Age: Best at 1–2 years, can go 3
Price: $6–10+
Recommended Producers: Angove's, Babich (NZ),

Brown Brothers E.B., Corbans Marlborough (NZ)
✪, Hill-Smith Fumé, Morton Hawkes Bay (NZ),
Nautilus ♦ (NZ), Roo's Leap Fumé, Rothbury Es-
tate, Taltarni

Foods: Spicy seafood, especially shellfish, gravlax,
goat cheese, salads with light vinaigrette or mus-
tard dressing

Proprietary Blends

Inexpensive blends with proprietary or brand
names are very popular in Australia. The country's best-selling single wine, reportedly, is Tyrell's Long Flat Red, mostly Shiraz smacked
with Cabernet and Malbec. This hearty red used
to go for something like $2.99 in the United
States, but now is up to $4.50 or $5. Still a Superbuy. Rosemount's Diamond Reserve Red,
about half Shiraz, half Cabernet, is also an excellent buy, but the Diamond Reserve White is
a Superbuy—mainly Hunter Valley Semillon
with a dash of Sauvignon Blanc to freshen it up.
Both, however, are a bit on the "mellow" side.

Age: Immediately drinkable
Price: $4–6.50
Recommended Producers: Hardy Premium Classic
Dry Red and Dry White, Rosemount Diamond
Reserve Red and White ✪, Tyrell's Long Flat Red
✪ and White

Rhine Riesling

The true German Riesling is called Rhine Riesling in Australia, occasionally Johannisberg
Riesling. Riesling is produced in great quantities
in Australia. Excellent Rieslings are made in the
Barossa Valley and Coonawarra, fresh, flowery,
delicate, and usually dry or off-dry. Relatively

little is exported to the United States because Rieslings are not appreciated here, but perhaps we will see more good Australian Rieslings in the future. Luscious late-harvest Rieslings are also made; affordable ones are listed under dessert wines.

Age: 1–2 years, can go longer
Price: $5–8
Recommended Producers: Jacob's Creek ♥, Penfolds Green Ribbon, Pewsy Vale ✪, Wynn's Coonawarra ✪
Foods: Poached or broiled fish, smoked salmon, cold chicken or turkey, chicken salad, pasta primavera, steamed asparagus with hollandaise or vinaigrette

---

Semillon

The white grape Semillon is not well known in the United States, particularly as a varietal, but it has long been one of Australia's most popular whites, and widely produced. The full-bodied, rich, oaky style of Semillon that is most favored was developed in the Hunter Valley (where it was once called, curiously enough, Hunter Riesling). In the United States and Bordeaux, Semillon is often blended with Sauvignon Blanc and is the principal grape used in Sauternes, but the style of Australian Semillon is unique. Ripe, full-flavored, somewhat honeyed in character, it served the role that Chardonnay played before it became widely planted in Australia. Like some of the moderately priced Chardonnays, Semillons are often rounded off with a bit of sweetness, but in well-balanced wines this does not hinder their palate-pleasing flavors or their ability to age five to seven years or longer. More

Chardonnay is imported from Australia than
Semillon.

Age: **Drinkable young, but good ones may not hit
flavor peak till 4 or 5 years, and hold a few be-
yond**
Price: **$5–10+**
Recommended Producers: **Henschke, Lindemans,
Penfolds Koonunga Hill, Rosemount Semillon/
Chardonnay ✪, Rothbury Estate, Tyrell's**

Shiraz

Shiraz, or Syrah, is sometimes labeled Hermitage in Australia in honor of the great Rhône
red of that name. Shiraz is the Persian name for
the Syrah grape, which is one of the world's
oldest. Australia's world-famous (and most expensive) red, Penfolds Grange Hermitage, is
made from Shiraz. The variety was first developed in the Hunter Valley, where producers
tried for the robust, powerful, almost burnt flavor of the Rhône's biggest reds—sometimes resulting in very brawny, alcoholic wines. Shiraz
is grown widely in Australia today, and the
modern style is for ripe, full-bodied but not
heavy reds, rich with the flavors of blackberries
or cassis. This is especially true of moderate-
priced Shiraz, which is often a remarkable bargain when the wines are good. More expensive
ones, such as Taltarni ($10), tend to be dark,
full-bodied, and tannic, needing a few years'
aging to be drinkable.

Age: **3–5 years, sturdy ones in price range may go
8–10**
Price: **$7–10**
Recommended Producers: **Bannockburn ◆, Brown**

Brothers, Leo Buring, Château Tahbilk, Hill-
Smith, Peter Lehmann ♥, Lindemans Bin 50,
Montrose, Rosemount Diamond Label, Rothbury
Estate Herlstone, Saltram Hazlewood, Seaview,
Seppelt Black Label, Taltarni ✺
Foods: Lamb or beef stew, game, savory cheeses
(goat cheese with the very berryish ones like Hill-
Smith)

Shiraz/Cabernet (See Cabernet/Shiraz)

Dessert and Fortified Wines

Australia has a long tradition of flavorful dessert and fortified wines, some of which are excellent value. Many of the late-harvest Rieslings
and Semillons, usually possessing the honeyed
flavors of Botrytised (noble rot) grapes, are lus-
ciously sweet and well balanced. Dessert Muscats, such as Brown Brothers Lexia or Mildara
Moscat Blanc, are exotic nectars that make a
wonderful finish to a meal.

The warm regions of central Australia, like
the Riverina district and regions along the Mur-
ray River, produce excellent fortified wines,
such as the very fine and very drinkable Yalumba Clocktower Port and Seppelt's Para Bin
110 Oloroso Sherry. In full bottles (750 milliliters), prices for good Ports and Sherry, as well
as late-harvest wines, have moved beyond $10,
but many of them are available in half-bottles
(375 milliliters, and so noted in the list below)
that are well within reach.

Age: Drinkable at release, but late-harvest wines
can age several years
Price: $7–10

Recommended Producers: **Brown Brothers Lexia ❂,
Heggies Botrytised Rhine Riesling (375), Mildara
Late Harvest Moscat Blanc, Penfolds Botrytised
Semillon (375), Peter Lehmann Vintage Port,
Pewsey Vale Botrytised Riesling ❂ (375), Seppelt
Show Muscat, Seppelt Para Bin 110 Show Olo-
roso Sherry, Yalumba Clocktower Port ❂ ◆**

SUPERBUYS / AUSTRALIA
AND NEW ZEALAND

White
Lindemans Chardonnay Bin 65, $6.50
Seppelt Reserve Bin Chardonnay, $8.99
Penfolds Koonunga Hill Semillon/Chardonnay,
$7.49
Rosemount Diamond Chardonnay, $7.50
Rosemount Chardonnay/Semillon, $7.50
Corbans Marlborough Sauvignon Blanc, $9
Pewsey Vale Riesling, $6
Wynn's Coonawarra Riesling, $6
Pewsey Vale Botrytised Riesling, $8.50
Brown Brothers Lexia Muscat, $7

Red
Penfolds Koonunga Hill Cabernet Shiraz, $7.49
Rosemount Diamond Reserve Red, $4.50
Tyrell's Long Flat Red, $4.50
Peter Lehmann Shiraz, $7
Taltarni Shiraz, $9
Montrose Shiraz, $7.99
Peter Lehmann Vintage Port, $9

Sparkling Wines

Most wineshops group sparkling wines together, since consumers usually want to peruse what's available. We often buy these wines based on price and style rather than origin, so instead of listing them within each country I thought it more useful to make them a category on their own.

There are dozens of sparkling wines for $10 and under, but not many that I can recommend for consistently good quality. Probably the overall best category for such wines are the Spanish *cavas*, which are made using a modified version of the traditional Champagne method. Most are made from the native Spanish grapes, Parellada, Xarel-lo, and Macabeo; some include Chardonnay and those that are 100 percent Chardonnay are more expensive.

Leading Champagne brands are at an all-time high, but some wineshops around the country bring in direct imports that can be inexpensive. Sparkling wines from the Loire, the Languedoc, the Jura, and Alsace can be quite good and a few are recommended below.

California has raised qualtity across the board for sparkling wines made by the *methode champenoise*—and several of the leading Champagne houses now have facilities in California—Moet, Roederer, Mumm, Deutz, Lanson, Taittinger, among others. At full markup California sparkling wines range from about $13 to $25. At certain times, however, various brands can be found marked down or featured as loss leader (♦) that put them occasionally within our range. It's rare with any of the French-owned but such as Korbel, Mirassou, Wente, Shadow Creek, or Domaine Chandon can be great value. Recommended below are sparklers from various parts of the world and the United States, all of which are dry except Asti (sweet Muscat from Italy's Piedmont) and Ballatore (Gallo's lightly sweet, semi-sparkling Muscat).

Age: **Immediately drinkable**
Price: **$7–10+**
Recommended Producers: **Ballatore ○, Bouvet Brut ♦, Brut Pecher, Charles de Fere, Chase-Limogère, Château Ste. Michelle Brut, Cinzano Asti Spumante, Codorníu Brut Classico ○ and Blanc de Blancs, Freixenet Brut Natur, Frescobaldi Brut, Gancia Pinot di Pinot and Gancia Asti ♦, Glenora Blanc de Blancs, Gratien & Meyer Brut and Blanc de Noir, Langlois Cremant Brut, Lembey Brut ○ and Premiere Cuvée ♦, Marqués de Monistrol, Monmousseau Sparkling Vouvray ♦, Masia Brut, Mont Marcal, Segura Viudas Blanc de Blanc, Valdivieso, Varichon & Clerc Savoir, Willm Cremant d'Alsace**

Glossary

Included here are brief explanations of some of the terms used in the text.

Auslese. German for late-harvest, usually Botrytis-affected grapes that produce luscious sweet wines.

Beerenauslese. Rare and expensive late-harvest sweet wine from bunch-selected grapes.

Blanco, branco. Spanish and Portuguese for white wine.

Botrytis cinerea. The mold that forms on grapes during harvest to produce luscious sweet wines; also known as "noble rot."

Cépage. Grape variety.

Clarete. Spanish for light red.

Crianza. Young wines aged only a year or two in cask; *sin crianza* signifies unaged wines.

Flash-pasteurizing. Subjecting a wine to a "flash" of high heat to prevent bacterial spoilage.

Garrafeira. Portuguese term for "personal or proprietor's reserve." Must be aged two years in wood, one in bottle before the wine is released.

Goût de terroir. French for the distinctive taste from a particular region or vineyard.

Grip. Wine-tasting term for a wine that has a firm thrust of fruit and tannin.

Halbtrocken, Trocken. *Trocken* is bone-dry, *Halbtrocken* is dry or off-dry in Germany.

Kabinett. Dry or off-dry German wines.

Négociant. Shipper or company who buys grapes or wine and sells under a brand name.

Plonk. Nondescript everyday wine.

Prädikat. The highest quality category for German wines, those with natural sweetness: Kabinett, Auslese, Beerenauslese, Trockenbeerenauslese.

Proprietary. Wines from a single proprietor, often with a brand name.

Qualitätswein. German term meaning "quality wine," but it's the designation for average to good wine.

Quinta. Portuguese for estate (*herdade* used in Alentejo).

Reserva, Gran Reserva. Spanish for superior wines, aged longer in cask and/or bottle.

Riserva. Italian for Reserve wines made from better lots and aged longer.

Rosado, Rosato. Rosé wine.

Rosso. Red wine.

Spätlese. Late harvest.

Tinto. Red wine.

Trockenbeerenauslese. Top quality level for rare, sweet German wines.

A Few Good Shops

Good wineshops and conscientious wine merchants have multiplied dramatically in the last decade. I have visited a good many and am on the mailing list of others, in an effort to keep track of wines available around the country. The following list is a selection of stores that I know personally to specialize in wine, offering diversity, good value, and good service. There are others, of course; I have not been to every state. Your local wine shop may well deserve to be here. But these stores are prototypes that typify the best in their area and are worth a visit if you are in the vicinity.

Atlanta: Skinflint's
Berkeley: Kermit Lynch
Boston: Brookline Liquor Mart; Cirace & Son
Chicago: Sam's Wine Warehouse; Schaefer's (Skokie); Knightsbridge
Covington, Ky.: Cork 'n Bottle
Dallas: Marty's
Detroit: Merchant of Vino
Fort Lauderdale: Crown Liquor
Ho-Ho-Kus, N.J.: Wine & Spirit World
Honolulu: Vintage Wine Cellar
Houston: Richard's
Kansas City, Mo.: Berbiglia; Gomer's

Los Angeles: Wally's; Trader Joe; Duke of Bourbon; Hi-Time Cellars (Costa Mesa); Wine Warehouse

Memphis: Buster's

Miami: Sunset Corners

Minneapolis: Haskell's

New Orleans: Martin Wine Cellar

New York City: Astor Wines & Spirits; Crossroads; Garnet; K & D; Morrell & Co.; Sherry-Lehmann; Heights Cellars (Brooklyn); Goldstar (Queens); Van Vleck (Brooklyn)

Westchester: Zachy's (Scarsdale); Rockwood & Perry (Hastings-on-Hudson)

Long Island: Pop's (Long Beach); Young's (Manhassett)

Upstate: Barbara's World (Albany); Century (Rochester); Premier Center (Buffalo)

Phoenix: Newman's Liquor Barn (Scottsdale)

Providence, R.I.: Town Wine and Spirits

Sacramento: Corti Bros.

St. Louis: Wine Cellar

San Francisco: The Jug Shop; Draper & Esquin; Liquor Mart; Cost Plus; Pacific Wine Co.

Bay Area: Beltramo's (Menlo Park); Mill Valley Market

Santa Barbara: Wine Cask

Seattle: Larry's Markets; Thriftway

Springfield, Mo.: Brown Derby

Washington, D.C.: MacArthur's; Pearson's; Calvert Woodley; Mayflower

Index

Notes

Notes

Notes

Notes